# Management Anecdotes

## By
## Vikram Khushalani

Learn Management through Anecdotes

# Dedication

*I humbly dedicate this book to all my Teachers.
My Parents being my first teachers.*

ISBN: 979-8-9888222-0-2 (Paperback)
ISBN: 979-8-9888222-3-3 (Paperback)
ISBN: 979-8-9888222-2-6 (Hardcover)
ISBN: 979-8-9888222-4-0 (Hardcover)


Library of Congress Control Number: 2023919332

# Contents

# Preface

**SOMEONE ASKED ME, IF I WERE STRANDED ON A DESERT ISLAND WHAT BOOK WOULD I BRING…'HOW TO BUILD A BOAT.'**
*~ Steven Wright*

As I was growing up I wish I had book, written by someone who wanted to share his or her experiences in life. How they negotiated the various turns of life. It did not matter which field they were in. All that mattered was that they would be willing to share their life experiences and the wisdom gained by them. In other words it would 'Show Me the Way'.

After I graduated and started working I came across some books by people who shared their life experiences. They were eye-openers. At least for me.

I could not have experienced life like that, at that early age. I am grateful to those people for having shared their life with the world.

This book is in that genera, as it attempts to share not only what has worked for me but in some cases, what has not. I do hope the readers of this book will benefit from my experiences, just as I benefitted from the books I read.

The book is based on factual anecdotes. Some names and gender may have been changed to protect the identity of those mentioned.

# Push the right buttons

## WE KNOW WHAT WE ARE, BUT KNOW NOT WHAT WE MAY BE
### ~ *William Shakespeare*

When I was in high-school, and getting ready to graduate, my father told me that he had set aside some money for me to either go to college or to start a business. He asked me what I wanted to do. For me, the choice was simple – Business. You see I did not want to study further, if I could help it. I could see that he was not thrilled with my response, but he said okay.

Being a writer, a language scholar, and a Civil Engineer, my father wanted all of his children to be college educated. My three elder sisters were working on their doctorates (one sister was studying to be a medical doctor), and my elder brother was studying to be a civil engineer. So my father used his knowledge of my nature, to psychologically redirect my decision. He knew that I was a 'neat' person and liked

cleanliness, so the following week he said 'You know –
Electrical Engineering is a very <u>neat and clean</u> profession'.
That got me thinking in that direction. He knew my buttons
and pushed one of the right ones.

A few days later he said 'Yes, business is a good idea, but
consider this – in business you have ups and downs. A
businessman, though he will never admit it, will always look
up to those who are educated'. And I, as a young man, was
trying to build my self-esteem and what I was hearing
sounded good to me

I ended up enrolling and ultimately getting a Bachelor's
Degree in Electrical Engineering. I have never regretted that.

**Push the Right Buttons**

As I look back to this incident I realized that one should look
for what motivates people, what are their innate
characteristics, what makes them happy, what they aspire for,
and provide them the way to achieve their goals. And in
turn, they will help you achieve your objectives.

This was just an early experience and an eye opener. Something I learned from and applied in my life later, at work and in social environments.

A child knows the body language of his/her parents. And also of other adults. They are innocent and can look through the façade we all build around us, they instinctively read our body language since they rely on it to interact with the world around them. As we grow older we lose that art, often because we lose our simplicity and innocence, and since we learn to mask our feelings and emotions. We learn from the society. And in the process we lose the ability to read body language.

A child knows what the buttons (so to speak) are of his /her parents. The child knows how to get attention and how to get what he/she wants from the parents.

As we grow older though, one has to be sincere, truthful, and above all empathetic to others. Help others achieve their short-term and long-term goals.

# Learn the Business

**I HATED EVERY MINUTE OF TRAINING, BUT I SAID, "DON'T QUIT. SUFFER NOW AND LIVE THE REST OF YOUR LIFE AS A CHAMPION"**
*~ Muhammad Ali*

Here I was – my first day at work. I had a college degree in Electrical Engineering and landed a job in the city's Power Plant. I was responsible for the installation of Heavy-Duty Electrical Transformers. I had the proud title of 'Supervisory Engineer' and I was assigned a team of 29 Technicians.

I had donned a suit and a tie – appropriate for my title and job. I was introduced to my team. My team comprised of people with various skill sets and levels, and some really senior and experienced staff.

After lunch I made my way gingerly to the work site and not having any practical experience, started questioning different staff members on what they were doing. This went on all afternoon, and also part of the day, next day. Shortly after lunch, one of my senior staff (who I learned later was a spokesman of sorts, for rest of the team) approached me and told me respectfully – 'Sir, you are new and seem to be getting in the way of our work. We have a deadline to meet, and if we do not meet it, you (as our supervisor) will take us to task. So, I have brought you your chair, so you can observe us from a close distance while we perform our tasks. Over time you will get it.'

I agreed, but as I sat on the chair observing them, I realized that if I was to supervise and lead them successfully, first - I would have to become one of them. I would need to learn the trade and earn their trust. I had to earn their respect, only then would I be able to contribute for the collective good of my project and my staff.

The next day I discarded the suit and showed up in work clothes. I was ready to roll up my sleeves and work with them on the floor. I called my staff and told them I was going to work side-by-side with each one of them, so I could learn what each one did. My team applauded my decision and I spent the next six-seven months working with them, learning, and also applying my education and individual knowledge to positively contribute to my project.

Soon after that, my team started seeking my advice and following my direction. Over time their respect for me grew to the extent that 2 years later, when the entire staff of the Thermal Power Plant went on strike for some issues, my staff showed up for work, since they did not want to let me down.

Realizing that their union had asked them not work, and they would be crossing the line with the union, thereby alienating themselves from the union and their co-workers, I had a meeting with my upper management. I suggested that I tell my team to join their co-workers to avoid jeopardizing their wellbeing and also to avoid conflicts within the workforce. This would also set a positive tone for negotiations with the union down the road. While everyone did not agree, the Chief Engineer saw benefit in my approach. This worked out well in the end since the Union realized that management did care for the workers.

I told my team to join their co-workers and support their union till things could be resolved between the Management and the union. This boosted my teams' morale and their trust for me even further. My team became the most cooperative, and efficient team. Worker absenteeism reduced and productivity was boosted.

One should not hesitate to wear the cloak of an apprentice to learn something new. People often try to hide their ignorance, so to speak, or lack of knowledge in any particular area. They feel that it will have a negative impact on their reputation. On the contrary I have seen that when one admits his/her ignorance in some area, people feel that the person is honest and willing to admit it. This builds their trust in the person, and when the person declares their expertise in another area, people are willing to listen.

I would often find out who has expertise in a particular field and then approach the person to learn from them or to solicit their help. This endears, in a way, the person to the seeker (in this case - it was me). They feel flattered that someone is leaning on their expertise for help. This makes the Subject Matter Expert more willing to impart the skill or to lend a helping hand.

It does not hurt to acknowledge that person's skill in that specific area. It bolsters them and, in turn, often makes your lack-of-knowledge, or skill, insignificant. Often one's esteem, in the eyes of others, grows.

Another source for information is Advertisements (Ads). Many times, the manufacturers provide some background information in an Advertisement of their product. This is true for any product. Therefore, when one is interested in say – Network Hardware, one can read up Ads on that area, on the internet. When one visits the site of the manufacturer, one can find additional information. One can enrich and add to one's knowledge. Then when one is doing comparison between different brands, one is better equipped.

One of my roommates in the second year of my engineering college (our engineering college used to assign 3 students per room in the first two years of our academic year) had a very high General Knowledge. He won the first prize in our

University, in the General Knowledge competitions. He won that honor for our college, four years in a row. He had knowledge of every subject. I asked him how he acquired that vast amount of knowledge. He confided that all he did was read Advertisements. He read Advertisements for every product, he also read brochures for travel, advertising the key attractions, flights, etc. Those were the days before the popularity of online systems and the internet. Those were also days when Advertisements carried more information than they do today.

So, if a person is interested in expanding one's horizons, one's knowledge, then Advertisements are still one very good source. One can even find tutorials on 'how-to' on vendor sites and other sites in general.

# Never say 'No'

**THERE IS NOTHING IMPOSSIBLE TO HIM WHO WILL TRY**
*~ Alexander the Great*

After working as an Electrical Engineer for over 5 years, I changed my career to Computer Programming, working for a Defense contractor. I was promoted to Project Leader after two years. It was a hands-on job, which entailed leading a team of programmers and also working with the government clients.

While the Project Manager was the one tasked with the responsibility of leading the overall project, I was responsible for 2-3 subtasks. The client would often communicate with me directly on those subtasks.

One day the client asked for some changes, just a week before the product was to be delivered. The product was already in integration testing. And the client wanted a functional change, which was not in the scope of the project.

I told the customer outright 'No'. He obviously was not happy and complained to the Project Manager (PM). The PM was smart and he told the customer that he would look into it and see what he could do. He also told him that if anything could be done, he would do it.

After we had conducted an impact analysis we went and discussed it with the customer and provided him the impacts and options. We also stated that in order to incorporate the functional changes he was requesting we would have to put forward a baseline change since it was out of scope and the cost would also increase. We also reminded him that the change would impact the delivery date of the product. We also requested that any change to scope/functionality asked for by the customer should come in writing from them, in the form of Change Requests. We ended the discussion with a willingness to accommodate any requested changes while following the process.

This made the customer realize the gravity of the issues and he was willing to step back and discuss the changes he was requesting internally, before formulating a Change Request. He asked us to continue on the current course and deliver the product as planned.

I learned a valuable lesson that one should never tell a customer an outright 'No'. That does not mean that you have to give in, even when you know you are right. One should provide an analysis of what the impacts would be, give the customer viable options and let the customer make the decision. Let the 'No' come from the customer.

There is always a better approach – one can say 'Let me look into it and I will get back to you with an answer. I will also discuss with ….."  And the person to discuss it with could be any stakeholder (remember our broader definition of Stakeholder).

NEVER SAY NO WHEN A CLIENT ASKS FOR SOMETHING, EVEN IF IT IS THE MOON. YOU CAN ALWAYS TRY, AND ANYHOW THERE IS PLENTY OF TIME AFTERWARDS TO EXPLAIN THAT IT WAS NOT POSSIBLE.

~ *Cesar Ritz*

# Bad news does not get better with time

HEADLINES, IN A WAY, ARE WHAT MISLEAD YOU
BECAUSE BAD NEWS IS A HEADLINE, AND
GRADUAL IMPROVEMENT IS NOT
~ *Bill Gates*

I was leading my first software project. Due to unforeseen circumstances one of the sub-contractors was running behind in delivering an integral module. This was going to impact the schedule. The sub-contractor promised additional resources to get back on track. Despite the additional resources the sub-contractor could not deliver on time.

I reviewed the Project Management Plan and Schedule and felt that if I could gain some time in the follow-on subtask, and the project could get back on track. Thinking that I still had time, I kept this to myself, not wanting to alarm the PM. I was quite certain this issue could be taken care of, provided…..provided…..

As it turned out, we lost some more time in the follow-on subtask and the project was further behind time. And to make matters worse for me, the PM learned about it from the sub-contractor. I was called to task.

I have Good news and Bad news.
The Good news is, we have been able to re-attach your severed hand......

The PM realized that my intentions were good, but asked me why I had not informed him earlier when I first learned that the project was at risk of being late. I told him that even though it was the sub-contractor whose module was late, I felt it reflected on me and I wanted to fix it before telling him. He told me 'always remember that - Bad News does not get better with time.' He added 'the sooner one knows about the problem the sooner one can go about fixing it'.

We did ultimately resolve the problem by 'fast tracking' two other follow-on tasks to execute them partially in parallel to gain some time. Which offset the delays caused by the upstream tasks earlier.

I have followed that rule and have seen that more often than not, early intervention helps the project.

# Plan … Plan … Plan

**POOR PLANNING ON YOUR PART DOES NOT CONSTITUTE AN EMERGENCY ON MINE**
*~ Bob Carter*

It has been wisely said 'Plan your Work and Work your Plan'. And we are always planning. Even if it is a small task, we plan it in our minds. Sometimes it is mentally - a visual approach, sometimes it is laid out more elaborately. Some people put the plan on paper. We always do plan.

I was a new manager in a company, and I had not planned out my approach fully. I had planned on when I would send the project to the Configuration Management Team. I had also planned when it would go into testing. I had not planned when I would send it to the Documentation Team. That was the usually omitted by a lot of managers.

Ray was the manager for the documentation team. When I approached him at the $n^{th}$ hour (so to speak), with a documentation request for the User Manual, he, very rightly got upset that I had not told him earlier, and was informing just before it was due.

The report also went to the Deputy Program Manager and the next thing I knew I was called in to justify why I had not planned it out. It was hard to explain, but in the end Ray was gracious to make his team work overtime to accomplish the task. For me it was a great lesson. A lesson I decided to incorporate in every detail.

I then started planning elaborately and creating detailed plans. I started getting all the departments involved in our weekly meetings and took everyone's input. As it is I was already sharing my Project Management Plan with upper management and our customer. But now I also included every stakeholder.

For every project and task - I also developed a Backup Plan, my Plan B. The backup plan included what we would do at every step if there was a hold-up. I, however, did not share this plan with every one, except key Stakeholders and got the customer's and upper management's concurrence and support on this Plan B. The key was not to slip past Key Schedule Dates.

I ensured that the Critical Path was never compromised (a critical path is the sequence of dependent tasks that form the longest duration, allowing one to determine the most efficient timeline possible to complete a project, as well as to determine the actual duration of the project based on all known variables). This way, the plan(s) were practical timetables for task completion.

I used to pull out the key dates from the Project Management Plan and would present those, as a Project Timeline, to all stakeholders, at periodic/regular meetings. This ensured that no-one was surprised. It ensured a smooth operation. It also ensured that everyone was informed and there were no surprises.

When we Plan our work, we have already put some thoughts in contingencies and what-ifs. Our tasks are smoothed out and if we need to use the 'Plan B' then we already have planned head start.

# Set a thief to catch a thief

### SET A THIEF TO CATCH A THIEF
### ~ *Callimachus*

When I was in school, I was roughneck. I also liked to play rather than study. The school principal retired and we got a new principal, who was from a military school. He was very strict, compared to the previous principal. He wanted his new school (our school) to be as disciplined as a military school.

He made sure that every student followed the school dress code. He made sure that students, particularly the boys, had their hair, cut to proper length. He would make random checks, walking through the assembled students in the morning (we used to have the entire school assembled, by class, every morning before the start of the school day for general prayers, announcements, etc.), to check proper and clean dressing, short - hand nails, etc. He also emphasized academics, rewarding those who did well in studies, had high attendance and were well behaved.

He also knew that there were students who would skip classes and go and hangout at nearby places. He called me (probably since I was one of the notable offenders), to his office and told me that he had noticed that I had leadership qualities, and he could help me achieve success in life by channeling my qualities in the right direction. He offered to make me a School Prefect, provided I made a sincere effort to mend my ways and become a model student for others to follow. He gave me a short time to think about it.

After some serious thinking, I felt that since I had 3 years to graduate from the school, this would probably be an opportunity to turn my academic life around. I agreed to his proposal, on the condition that he would not expect me to snitch on my fellow students. He said 'Fine – as long as you uphold school discipline and rules, and … and influence your fellow students to do the same'.

I started enjoying my newfound authority, some privileges (like not only representing the school to my fellow students, but also being able to represent my fellow students to the school authorities), and above all some respect and leniency from the teachers towards me. And being a School Prefect, I had to mend my ways and start monitoring others to follow school rules.

I am pretty sure that the principal kept a close watch, though from a distance, over my behavior and activities. He called me in after 3-4 months and asked me to help the school, and help those specific students who skipped classes and hung out outside the school while the school was in session. He said the he was not interested in punishing those students as long as they mended their ways. And he gave me a free hand for a month, to see if I could reduce this absenteeism.

**Set a thief to catch a thief**
-Callimachus

He was smart – he knew that being an offender in the past I knew those students and spots where they hung out. Well I did know and went to work on this persuading 60% of the students to stop skipping classes during school. So, he improved this situation of absenteeism by 'Setting a thief to catch a thief' so to speak.

It has been said 'The lessons of childhood are not easily forgotten'. I have not forgotten this wisdom.

# How I became a Consultant

**A CONSULTANT IS SOMEONE WHO TAKES YOUR WATCH AWAY
TO TELL YOU WHAT TIME IT IS
~ Ed Finkelstein**

I had been working as an employee, for a company, for almost five years. I felt that I was not being recognized for my true worth. I felt I was being taken for granted, more so since the company management probably felt that I was not going to go anywhere else. I felt that I had reached the end of my progress with that company.

One day I saw an advertisement in the Employment Section of the Post, a Consultant recruitment company was looking for new consultants. They had clearly mentioned that the candidates should not have been a consultant before. They were looking for fresh blood, fresh talent.

In those days (of yore) there were a very few consultants in the market. Most of them were known in the Technical industry. Most of the corporate recruiters knew which consultant to call for which technical issue. So this Consultant recruitment company was trying to draw out new people. They would then, turn around and offer those candidates to their clients as new talent. And since they were 'new consultants' their charge rates would be much lower.

I jumped at the opportunity, went for my interview, and landed my first consulting assignment. And I enjoyed it from day-one. I enjoyed it for four reasons:

- The earnings were much higher
- Since this was purely for money, every day, at the end of the day, when I left my client's office – I left the worry of my work behind
- If my client asked me to work longer hours – I got paid for the extra time I spent working
- There was more technical respect – I was considered an expert in my field

There were disadvantages though:

- There were dry periods, in between assignments
- It was like a Taxi Meter – if you did not work, there was no pay
- You did not get paid 'Sick Leave' or 'Vacations'

- When you were not working – you could not foretell how long the dry spell would continue

Before I became a consultant, I heeded the advice of other consultants – always save three month's salary/expenses for the dry periods. I got Liability Insurance.

I had also discussed with my wife all these issues and we were both on board with the risks and the expected 'down periods'. We made sure that she carried the family's Health Insurance.

I learned a lot about how a small business runs. About taxes being different. About marketing, about contracts, etc. I also learned that one has to walk away from a 'what appears to be lucrative offer, but it fraught with risk'.

I also learnt that during economic downturns, consulting jobs are scarce. One has to go back to being an employee. And consulting does not always pay-back if one wants to rise in the corporate world.

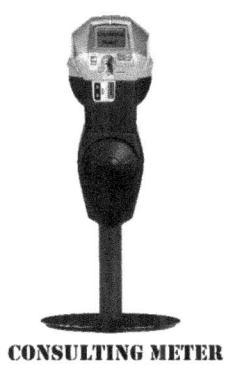

**CONSULTING METER**

Often – I would get job offers from my clients. I turned down many such offers, and later, regretted turning down some others.

I have also landed jobs, when the times were hard and job offers from my clients were timely and reasonable.

I also learnt some valuable skills on dealing with people.

Another thing I learned was to evaluate the effort needed for a task, job, or a project, with reasonable accuracy. Also to cost it out for myself and for my clients. And to evaluate risks and their mitigations, and to plan for those for my tasks and projects.

I also learned to identify the stakeholders and their areas of interest and influence. I dealt with stakeholders, who were at various corporate or client levels. And to address the needs of each stakeholder accordingly.

# You get paid, only after I get paid

**YOU MAY NOT GET WHAT YOU PAID FOR, BUT YOU WILL PAY FOR WHAT YOU GET**
*~ Maya Angelou*

During my consulting days, and during one of my dry spells (in between my consulting jobs) – I was not on a contract and I was looking for my next opportunity. As I scanned the employment section of the newspaper for project leads, I saw a small advertisement from a company asking for help for their Oracle Database. It was a very short-term assignment. Normally I never went for short-term contracts, I usually preferred a minimum of 3 month contracts. However, in this case I was looking for any contract, so I contacted them.

An appointment was setup for the same day. The company owner told me, on the phone, that they needed help immediately since their database was down. They did have a number of Oracle developers but this was beyond their skill set. I agreed to meet with the owner.

I showed up that afternoon. It was a small company and they were sub-contracting with a bigger company for managing the Oracle Database and to do some development work.

It was an office with three rooms. On one end was the room which was the company owner's office. It had one window. Next to that was a much larger room, with no windows. It had three doors, one door being the main entrance door to the company. All the staff was situated in this room. The other door in this office led to the computer room, which housed the database servers. The computer room did not have any windows either.

I was led to the owner's office. We discussed the issues the company was having. The company owner asked me if I had any ideas on how to resolve their issues. I suggested giving him half an hour free, to log in to their servers and assess the issues and let him know whether I can resolve it or not. That was fair and he agreed.

I then determined within 15-20 minutes what their issue was and told him that I felt I could help them and that I could get them up and running the next day and then it might take me two more days to do cleanup, backups, etc. He was very happy and we went back to his office and negotiated the terms of the contract, including my hourly fees. We decided it would be a three day contract.

He asked me to wait in the main room (where all the staff sat) for the contract to be worked on and prepared for signatures.  It took about half an hour for the contract to be prepared (from their template).  His secretary then brought it to me for my signature.  It was 4 page contract.  I told them I would like to read it.

They asked me to sign it at that time.  They said that they will, of course, provide me a copy and I could read it at home.  I told the owner that I always prefer to read it 'before' I signed it. They reluctantly agreed, since they had no choice in the matter.

I read the contract fully, word-for-word, since I was alerted by their hurry for me to sign it.  Everything was in order, except one sentence (from my point of view). The sentence was:

"The consultant will get paid, after we get paid by our client."

This sentence was not unusual in large Government Contracts.  It was, however, unusual in small contracts.  And more so since I was a consultant whom they were hiring for a short time.

I asked them that to remove the sentence, before I signed the contract.  I said 'I would like to be paid for the services I provide, as per the contract, within 15 days of submitting my invoice.  I added that it is the cost of doing business, which bigger (than me – a consultant) companies can survive.  I am a consultant, a small corporate entity, at the end of the food chain, and I cannot sustain a delay in payment.

The owner of the company refused, saying this is a contract they had always used and they would not change it. I asked him to re-consider his decision. He told me his decision was final.

I thanked him for his time, and picked my brief case, and headed for the door. He was not expecting this. He quickly ran to the door, and blocked my exit. He told me very politely that he had re-considered and would make the change to the contract.

The change was made. I signed the contract. Received a copy and was ready to leave the office.

Before I left the office, he asked me to also teach his senior Oracle developer, how to take care of the database. I told him that I will be glad for his senior developer to watch, over my shoulder, to see what I was doing, and to ask questions. However, I was being hired to fix the issue. Training cannot be achieved in such a short time. If he wanted to train his employee(s) on managing the database, then we could either modify the contract, or write another contract for training.

I suggested that I would give his staff some pointers on how to keep the database up.  They would be just pointers.  He would be better either hiring a Database Administrator or sending his selected staff for such training.

I showed up early the next day.  By the end of a long 10 hour day, I was able to resolve their issue, cleanup the server, back it up and start a daily backup of the server.  I showed his staff how to restore their database, in case of an issue.

I told the owner that my work was done.  He was very happy to shave two days off of the contract and save some money.  We both parted happy with the results.

This incident added to my experience with contracts.  And also reinforced some approaches I was developing towards contract negotiations and contract management.

I decided that the while the payment clause cannot be helped where one is a prime contractor for the government, however it can be influenced where the government contracting officer has some leeway in contracting, particularly when the contract is small.  Even as a company/contractor working for a bigger company, one need not be tied to when the bigger company gets paid.  In commercial contracting one can negotiate when one gets paid.

And when I was working for bigger company, and I was responsible for hiring the services of a smaller, or skillful in a 'particular area' company.  Or even when hiring a consultant.  I did look after the interest of the smaller guy, if I could help it.  It is the only fair way of dealing with others.

# Tell them what you are going to tell them

### TELL THE AUDIENCE WHAT YOU'RE GOING TO SAY, SAY IT; THEN TELL THEM WHAT YOU'VE SAID
### ~ Dale Carnegie

When I was working at International Business Machines (IBM), all the meetings required presentations. Those were the days before the Microsoft PowerPoint program popularity. All presentations were done with 'Transparencies'. We had 2-3 internal meetings every week and had to prepare the Transparencies for each meeting. During the meeting we would operate the transparency projector to present our material.

While developing and preparing the transparencies we would make changes, edits, updates, etc. It was time consuming and one would have to feed blank transparency sheets into the printer in order to print a set, for dry-runs, meetings, etc.

While this was cumbersome and sometimes even burdensome, I welcomed the need to do the presentations. It got us into the practice of doing presentations, such that when we did presentations to our customer weekly, we were so used to doing presentations that it was no sweat.

I developed a how-to methodology for presentations I will share later in this chapter. I want to mention a few points first:

When developing or preparing a presentation on a subject, one should research the subject to the best of one's capability, in the time available. This allows one the luxury of tailoring the presentation for the best impact. This research will also help one to answer questions during or after the presentation.

With regards to the topic of the presentation – ask yourself whether you are the Subject Matter Expert (SME) on the topic. Are you the right person to give the presentation? If not – get the right person to give the presentation (if that is possible). Or have the right person sitting in the audience to address questions or details. The right person could be someone on your staff, your team, your project, or even a guest. Use your best judgment.

The next suggestion depends on the intended impact of the presentation. Often it is better to run the draft of the presentation by your client, or the decision maker, ahead of time. Get their buy-in and the presentation will go smoother.

Another approach that has worked well for me is to ask the client/decision-maker/stake-holder, whether they would like to include a slide in the presentation, so they can address it? This will give them a feeling of ownership and they will treat the presentation as their own, and even defend it – if need be.

Now here is the approach, how-to methodology, I developed for effective presentations:

- **Tell them what you are going to tell them**
- **Tell them**
- **Tell them what you just told them**

In other words - In slide No. 2, give an overview of what you are going to present. In subsequent slides provide your material. In the next to last slide, synopsize what you presented (this is, so that they remember the primary presentation).

So, what about the first and the last slides? The first slide can hold the title (to include subject, contract number, etc.) and the presenter-and-client counterpart's name and titles. The last slide should have text stating the End/Questions, thus indicating the conclusion of the presentation and inviting questions or discussion from the attendees.

Include some slides with graphics. They are pleasing to the eyes and can convey ideas vividly. Graphics can be art, or diagrams, charts, tables, flow diagram, or even photographs. And if the presentation is part of a regular or periodic series of presentations then you graphic slide(s) can also be updatable.

Another suggestion is to put just a few bullets on each slide. Too many bullets could make the presentation look too busy. Adding enough white space around the text is also less taxing on the eyes.

This approach also works very well with a speech or a talk. Though do not give away the punch lines in the beginning. Save it for the appropriate time.

It is important that the level of detail in the presentation, or talk, suits or meets the need of the audience. As an example one will synopsize the subject matter at a higher level for upper management. On the other hand architects and engineers may want more details. So, give the audience what they want and will remember.

There is a caution though – it is best not to make the presentation very long and best not to stuff too many topics in a presentation. The presentation should have one primary, or over-arching, theme for it to be effective and remembered.

One final suggestion – it works very well to engage the audience in your presentations. They will not forget it. For example if you know people in your audience you can call them out 'Bob, this slides will be interest to you', or 'Jack this slide answers the question you had the other day'. Even if you do not know your audience, like I have had occasion to address, you can say something like – 'What I am about to tell you next will appeal to the folks who ask..., or who always do ...' etc.

I later discovered that in Advertising, they use/repeat information three times also. The Advertising rule of thumb is that you repeat important information three times. Their research has shown that this way a person remembers the information. And that is what we are doing here.

So, remember to -
- **Tell them what you are going to tell them**
- **Tell them**
- **Tell them what you just told them**

# Meetings

A MEETING IS AN EVENT AT WHICH THE MINUTES
ARE KEPT AND THE HOURS ARE LOST
~ *Unknown*

A lot of people do not like office meetings.  And for good reason – a mismanaged meeting can end up wasting one's time.

There should be a specific goal for every meeting.  And one should structure the meeting so that the goal is achieved. For example, if it is a regular staff meeting then it should meet its stated agenda.  If it is an informational meeting then the stated information should be disseminated.  If it is one of a kind, even then it should meet its agenda.

Where feasible, very one, or every entity, should be get an opportunity to contribute to the meeting, even the 'nay' Sayers. For unless we hear from all sides, of the house (so to speak) we may not be able to make the right choices, of provide the needed information to all.

Whether it is an informal meeting, or a formal one, all participants, invitees, and stakeholders should have a say.

I found it best to distribute the meeting topic, purpose, agenda, and venue ahead of time, so people can plan attendance and participation. When the purpose of the meeting was to get approval, concurrence, or active participation of stakeholders, I would have discussions (time permitting) with the stakeholders ahead of time, get their feedback and recommendations and/or concurrence so I could seal it formally during the meeting.

I would sometimes send out drafts of the agenda, and meeting material ahead of time so I could get stakeholder thoughts, and if possible, their concurrence ahead of time. This way I would avoid wasting everyone's time and still achieve the purpose of the meeting.

Everybody's time and opinion is valuable. So, I would start the meeting by noting down the attendees, and from time-to-time turn to them for their opinion. Sometimes I would ask the opinion of the stakeholder even when they were antagonistic to the meeting's anticipated goal. This would, in many situations, disarm the objections of the stakeholder. Or there would be others, in the meeting, who could provide solutions to the stakeholder's issues.

Make sure to go around and ask each attendee if they have anything to add or comment on. In case the meeting exceeds manageable number of participants, conclude the meeting with 'Are there any questions from anyone?'

Make sure that if there are action items resulting from the meeting, that they are reiterated for every one's benefit and the owners of the action items are aware of the due-dates for completion, or updates.

I would often encourage stakeholders to include a slide or two in my meeting presentations so they felt committed and contributed to the common goal. This would also lend greater legitimacy to the presentation and underscore the importance of the subject matter. It would also convey concurrence from the stakeholders and most importantly – provide the stakeholder a platform to address the issue and feel important and committed to the common goal.

Remember to send out the minutes, important decisions reached, action items and their due-dates to all invitees, and all attendees (there have been occasions when some attendees have not been invited, but one of the stakeholders invited them to attend) and any other stakeholder you feel should be informed or involved.

Most importantly – keep the meetings short and to the point, unless it is a working meeting. The format of working meetings is different and they can be lengthy. For a working meeting – identify and formulate the goal of the meeting and its timing, where relevant. Working meetings can also be brown-bag (attendees bring their lunch) or one can cater lunch or snacks.

The meetings I attended with the Civil Aviation Authority (CAA) [The CAA is the British Government's Aviation Authority, just like the Federal Aviation Authority (FAA) of

United States] in London, were both – a status meeting and a working meeting.

The British often have Tea around 3:30 – 4:30 PM.  And the meetings were no exception.  So, around that time in the evening they would provide Tea and Biscuits to all attendees.  This would perk attendees up.

When conducting or attending meetings - give importance and respect to all.  Acknowledge all entities and ensure that everyone's relevant issues, topics, and opinions are either addressed or scheduled for future meetings.  Try to get active participation from everyone.  This applies to face to face meetings, as well as conference call, and remote attendees.

# One on one

**IT'S A PRIVILEGE TO BE IN THIS POSITION, TO HAVE PEOPLE WANT TO TALK TO ME, TO HAVE PEOPLE WANT TO HEAR MY STORY AND HEAR WHAT'S GOING ON, BECAUSE IT CAN EASILY BE ON THE FLIP SIDE, AND NO ONE WANTS TO TALK TO ME, NO ONE RESPECTS ME ONE-ON-ONE, NO ONE IN THE STANDS WEARING MY JERSEY. IT'S A BLESSING.**
*~ Deshaun Watson*

I learnt a very important lesson from Marv. He was a manager who had a very unique trait. Whenever someone went to talk to him, on any subject – he would give his full attention to that person. He would put down his pen, he would put down his papers, and he would turn away from his computer screen (if he was using his computer) and pay full attention to you.

He would then listen to what you had to say. He would be attentive to every word you said. He would interact actively with you.  He would take time to think over what you had said and he would make comments, suggestions and discuss the issues you had brought up.  He would be willing to consider any suggestion you made and would discuss alternatives with you.  He would be a keen participant in the conversation with you.

This made one feel important and listened to.  It made you feel that he was there to listen to you, to address your issues, and you were talking to him one-on-one.  And it conveyed the feeling that what you had come to say was important enough for him to listen with undivided attention.

When I adopted this habit too – I realized that it was I who benefited from this the most.  I was able to give my full attention to matters in a timely fashion and also leave the other person with the feeling of importance, being heard, and a sense of fulfillment.

ONE ON ONE

---

Often when someone has come to talk about some grievance, or to complain about something – paying full attention to them and listening to them will, more often than not, calm them down.  I would also gain insight, by listening, and looking at visual clues, observing the other person's demeanor.  This may not be possible if one does not pay full attention to the person.  Or if one is engaged in some other activity while talking – like looking at your papers, shuffling them.  Or staring at your computer screen while conversing with the person.

Treat the person who has come to you with respect and dignity.  Treat them like you would when a senior corporate officer stops by to chat with you.  Do not forget that if you were visiting someone, you would like to be treated with respect for your opinion and yourself.

This approach also establishes a communication bond with the person you are interacting with.   People will not forget you, as I have not forgotten Marv.

# Honesty is the Best Policy

**BEING HONEST MAY NOT GET YOU A LOT OF FRIENDS BUT IT'LL ALWAYS GET YOU THE RIGHT ONES.**
*~ John Lennon*

Ethics should play the central role in one's endeavors. When we cultivate an ethical way of life, it will reflect in everything we do. This is true of every aspect of life – even the mundane ones. And honesty is the most important, and fundamental, factor in any relationship. It should be a keystone of one's management methodology and practice.

One has to cultivate ethical behavior. This may seem difficult in a business environment, but once you are known for your ethical dealings it becomes easier. A person known for his/her ethics is trusted. The person becomes valuable in any dealing, but even more so in 'high stakes' dealings. Oh, there will be challenges, but one will develop strength and get help from symbiotic forces. This has been experienced firsthand, by me, many times.

A Gold Medal winning article my father once wrote was titled 'Utility of Honesty in Trade'. And he lived that life and as such was highly respected by his peers, superiors, and all those around him. He endeavored to instill those very principals in all his children.

I was a project leader at a software company and was considered a highly promotable employee. One day the Executive VP called me into his office and told me so too. He praised me highly and said he would like to share something with me. He walked over to his filling cabinet, unlocked it, and pulled out a thin file binder. He said 'I am going to share some information with you'. And rolled his chair in front of me.

I felt, rightly or wrongly, that something was not quite right in this picture. And I did not want to get into a situation where things could head south. He was overacting or was under stress. So, I told him 'The Company can trust me, I have been brought with a strong sense of Morality and Ethics, and I do not compromise in that regard, so I will not do anything that is not right. You can trust me in that regard.'

Hearing this, his tone and attitude changed. He then started taking about various other things and the company's future in general terms. And while doing all the talking, he casually put the file back into his filling cabinet. He then continued talking for a while and finally thanked me for all my good work and shook my hands and walked me to the door of his office. Mentally I heaved a sigh of relief and walked back to my office.

My suspicions were indirectly confirmed and where he used to be friendly and chat with me in the hallway, he now avoided me, except to briefly nod a hello. I also observed that what used to be my rapid growth in the company came to a standstill. And believe me, I was very happy to have not been shown that file. As some say – the best way to win a war is to avoid it. And I did not feel that my progress at that company was a make-or-break for my career. Whereas a compromise on my ethical beliefs would have been a break (like in broken) for my life.

I did finally move on to another company to pursue my career growth.

Ethics and Honesty also mean doing the right thing for your clients, for the stakeholders (to include the company you work for), your peers, and your staff. As human beings, we all move individually, and we move together, as a society. In helping others, we help ourselves. In looking after others, we look after ourselves. If we do things only for ourselves, if we are selfish in our motives, we may have a short-term gain, but we will have a long-term loss.

The Golden Rule stated by Jesus in Luke 6:31 "Do to others as you would have them do to you." And in Matthew 7:12 "So, in everything, do to others what you would have them do to you, for this sums up the Law and the Prophets."

This, I believe, is the starting and motivating point of Ethics and Honesty – Doing to others what you want others to do to you. The other point is 'compassion'. One has to have compassion and empathy for others.

# Say what you <u>will</u> *do* and *Do* what you said you <u>would</u>

**WHEN YOU SAY YOU WILL DO SOMETHING AND YOU DON'T DO IT, YOU TEACH OTHERS (INCLUDING YOURSELF) THAT YOU CANNOT BE TRUSTED.**
*~ Unknown*

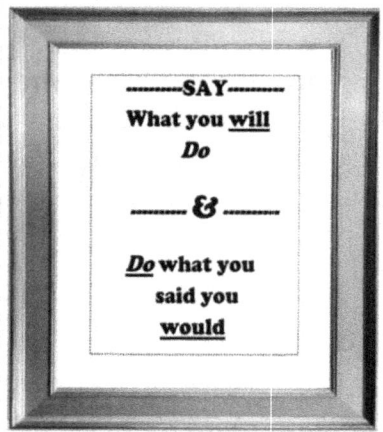

Your word is your promise.  When we commit to do something we should follow through and do everything in our power to accomplish it.  Once we adopt this approach and start practicing it, others will take notice and start believing our word.

This is very important in our dealings, in our relationships, and in Project Management.  One should not commit to what is not feasible.  One should tell it the way it is.  One <u>can</u> commit to doing the best of one's capability, or 'circumstance permitting', though one may not have that luxury on a project. In which case one has to come up with a good estimate on what it will take to complete a task.

In order to arrive at a solid estimate, use your own experience, coupled with the experience of experts. So who are the experts? For a coding task it will be people who know how to code, and also software engineers and architects. For tasks relating to construction it could be the person who is involved day-to-day in hands-on construction.

Do not forget to include and incorporate estimates from testers, integrators, the quality assurance team, the integration team, the configuration management team, any vendors or contractors supplying you products or services.

Once one has arrived at a good task-estimate, taking factors mentioned (and some others one can think of situationally), one can then add a percentage for unforeseen circumstances, or what some people refer to as a 'fudge factor'. Factor that into the final estimate as a 'margin of error'. And let it be known that you have done so. Keep everything above board and transparent.

Also make sure that you have listed the contingencies, risk factors, and dependencies. Try to assess the impacts of all these factors on the project. Remember that your staff has to believe in the feasibility of the plan. Once your assessment is completed and finalized in your mind, commit to the plan.

Share your commitment with all stakeholders, get it blessed by the powers who have the authority. Start the execution of the plan.

Monitor your project closely and make every effort to deliver as promised. Keep all stakeholders informed and abreast of the progress. If there are problems or delays then inform your stakeholders immediately. This builds stakeholder confidence in you. Problems and issues are part of the life of a project. By keeping all stakeholders informed you build their confidence and trust in you. This will pay dividends and contribute to your credibility over time.

On a parallel note – if you feel from the get-go that a project/task has potential issues then tell your stakeholders what those issues are, or that it cannot be done. They may not like your answer and this may affect you in the short term but at least you are not setting yourself up for failure.

As an example - I was working as an IT consultant for a company which maintained a large member database of two competing organizations. The database was maintained in a product called FOCUS [which was a fourth-generation programming language (4GL) - originally developed for data handling and analysis on the IBM mainframe] by Information Builders, Inc. (IBI)]. This company I was consulting with, was facing a slowing data-retrieval process, as its client membership (read as data-records) grew in number. So they hired my services, since I was a FOCUS developer also, to look into the problem and resolve it.

After running some tests, and applying some efficiencies, re-running the tests I realized that the data system FOCUS had reached its limit (in that version) and was therefore slowing record-retrieval down.

I informed my client that the system had reached its limit and suggested they use an IBM product – Virtual Storage Access Method (VSAM), which had greater scalability and capacity. I also told them that if they approved the approach

I could build a small prototype and we could compare the results.

The client was not convinced and instead called FOCUS directly and asked them to send in their consultant to review the problem. The FOCUS consultant came and told the company that I did not know what I was talking and that they would be able to resolve the issue.

I was told to leave, which I did gladly since I knew the issue could not be resolved with the system they were using.

One month later the client called me, he first apologized for their asking me to leave, saying the FOCUS consultant had tried and failed and had even made the system slower. They then requested me to go back and help them. I told them that I would let them know since I was helping another client. In the meantime I gave it some serious thought and decided to go back and restore my reputation with them fully. But before I could call them, they called again - so I agreed.

I was able to build a prototype in VSAM and confirm my initial analysis and then built the new system for them, which was much faster and had some useful utilities to back up and restore their systems.

I learnt later that future releases of FOCUS had resolved those issues with data retrieval latency.

# Be Transparent, but do *not* wear Invisible clothes

### BE TRANSPARENT, NOT SEE THROUGH
*~ Julian Hall (ultrapreneursayings.com)*

THE EMPROR'S NEW CLOTHES

During a re-compete, the company I was working for lost the contract we were on. The winner of the contract was a smaller company and they won on price, and a promise of a better performance. The owner of the company, which had won the contract, knew me through my work there and had talked to me a couple of times since he had consulted for the end client. He had convinced the end client, I think, that he could save them money and still provide them the same, or better, performance. He went about hiring key staff of the losing company, as is often the case.

He offered me a job, however I was not interested in working for a smaller company, at that time. I was not sure that the smaller company would be able to sustain itself beyond the currently won contract. Besides, I had other plans. I wanted to get back into consulting, and wanted to transition out of the employee status I held.

Since the corporate client liked my work and I had a good working relationship with the client staff, including the Project Manager, I thought I would explore the possibility of working directly with them as a consultant.

So, I approached the client's Corporate Human Resources department and asked them for, and filled out, forms declaring myself as a small operator, and awaited the results. The Human Resources department got back to me within a fortnight and put me on their bidders list.

I then bid for an open sub-section of the technical portion of the contract. I declared myself a Subject Matter Expert (SME) on that section due my experience and expertise in that subject area. I stated my fees and conditions and also approached the Chief of the Department and let the Chief know that I had submitted a bid for that sub-section.

I also attended a bidder's meeting and met again with the Chief. After several rounds I was assured a consulting contract based on my experience with the subject matter and skills. It was just a matter of time and formality for my paperwork to come through.

While I was waiting, and wanting to be transparent, I called the owner of the smaller company which had won the general contract and told him that this was happening and that I would be fully cooperative with his staff and we could work together.

Well – that was the wrong move on my part. While the owner was very nice on the phone and looked forward to working together, he approached the Chief, Project Manager, and whoever he could, and stopped the issuance of my contract.

I realized that, in this case, I was not just transparent, perhaps I was too transparent – like almost wearing invisible clothes. Lesson Learned.

So, while it is good to be transparent, with respect to your projects, with your stakeholders. It was not good to be too…too, transparent. Remember that my definition of stakeholders is very broad. So, it behooves us to be transparent for the sake of honesty and for the fact that being transparent avoids future grief and the need to explain things later. Being transparent allows us to have everyone on the same page, in more ways than one.

It is presumptuous to think that everyone we meet, in the corporate world, has the same value system as us. So, one has to be very careful, on a personal level, as to how transparent one can be. When it comes to a personal level, one owes it oneself to uphold one's benefit, as long as it is ethical and it does not hurt others in the grand scheme of things.

So, looking back at my call to the owner of that company, it would have been better not to call him. He would have found out, sooner or later, after I had got my contract papers. Finding out later would not have undermined his contract, since this was an open sub-area, for which I had bid.

---

# Beware of the Office-Snitch

### LOOSE LIPS MAY SINK SHIPS
*~ From a World War II poster by Seymour R. Goff*

## BEWARE THE OFFICE SNITCH
## IT CAN "SNIFF OUT" NON-ISSUES

Most offices have a person, or two, who behave like 'Snitches'. This undermines sincere people's effort. Such people get ahead in life by telling on others. And such behavior is often condoned by the people, whose ear they have. Those people often do not realize that the 'Snitch' can act against them also, with their superiors, if the Snitch got an opportunity to do so.

Some of these people will also manufacture stuff (imaginary things) when they run out of material. They do not want to diminish their information potential for their audiences. This works against others trying to do their level best at their jobs. They become victims of manufacture lies.

There was such a person on one of my contracts. He would always look for an opportunity to show others in poor light. He would transgress the Point of Contact (POC) etiquette of the Program/Project Culture. This often undermined the Company's Projects and Programs. He would go and spill the beans on project internals, whether they were schedule, budget, risk, and etc. related. While this was condoned by the Senior Managers, since they thought they had a well-placed informant, it went against the company since this person was very vocal with the clients, even to the detriment of the company.

As it is, I was always upfront and transparent with my client POC. This, however, made me vigilant, particularly since it affected what was over-heard by this Snitch. This person would also go and talk to my client POC, against our projects.

It did not affect our projects, since the client was always aware of potential issues and our efforts to resolve them. Except one time, when it was breaking news by our developers/engineers regarding an issue which had just surfaced. Even as I called a meeting to handle the issue, the client showed up at the door of my office and asked me about the issue. He told me that the Snitch (he of course did not refer to the person as such) had just told him.

I invited him to sit at the meeting, with all of us. The meeting was about to start. Our Senior Project Engineers and Architect were headed to my office. I was amazed at the speed this Snitch worked though.

The client sat down with us, but left shortly, after satisfying himself that things were under control, as usual. He trusted us since I was open with him and told him that this issue had just surfaced and we were going to discuss the cause, effect, and resolution approach.

Unfortunately, such people are almost everywhere in large projects. This should make us resolve that one's behavior and ethics should be unquestionable. We should always keep all stakeholders in the loop. Remember that being open and keeping everything above-board will keep you out of the hot water. It will keep you free from undue worries.

Remember that in the end, the Snitch is also you stakeholder. The person has an undue, though un-healthy, interest in your project. Keep the person at longer-than-arm's-length from your project and from your staff, where possible.

When you make an effort to start identifying your stakeholders, make an effort to also identify such people. These people are stakeholders with a negative stance towards your projects and staff. Just be pleasant and keep them at a safe distance from your interests. And be discrete in sharing their identity with your staff and your colleagues.

# Stakeholders

**TELL ME AND I WILL FORGET
SHOW ME AND I MAY REMEMBER
INVOLVE ME AND I'LL UNDERSTAND.**
*~ Chinese Proverb*

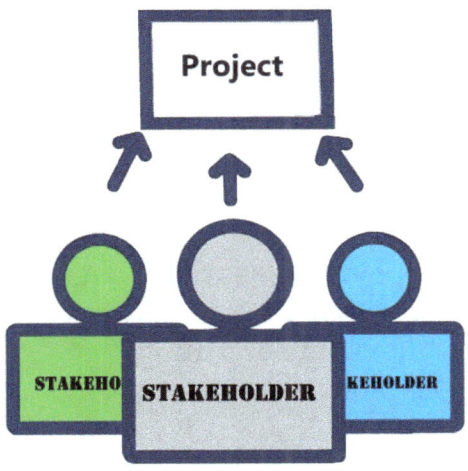

Do you know who the stakeholders are for you project?

According to the 5th edition of the PMBOK® Guide a *Stakeholder is an individual, group or organization who may affect, be affected by, or perceive itself to be affected by a decision, activity or outcome of the project.* So, do you know you're your stakeholders?

I realized that my team (who was working on the project) was the most critical, and the most important group of stakeholders, followed by me (the successful outcome of the project was my primary job as the project manager), then came my enabling client (for whom the project was undertaken), and so on. The key was that the people who make it happen were the ones most effective and the ones most affected by the outcome of the project. They lived and breathed the project on a day-to-day, hour-to-hour basis. So, it is important that they realize their importance and take ownership of the project. They succeed when the project succeeds.

One must convey this to the team. Every successful project is another feather in their cap. And every project is new, unique (per definition in the PMBOK: A project is a temporary endeavor undertaken to create a unique product, service or result), and will add to the experience of the team.

For the team – the customer is King. In the old days – when the King was pleased he would reward his subjects. When the customer is happy, he/she will find a way to send additional contracts your way. And for this reason – for the Company also – the customer is King.

**STAKEHOLDER REQUIREMENTS**

All stakeholders are important. The ones who influence the outcome of a project, and the ones who are influenced by the outcome of the project.

So, find out all the obvious stakeholders and also the non-obvious ones. The non-obvious stakeholders could become your future stakeholder. So, identify all of your project stakeholders.

Once you have identified the list of your project stakeholders, ensure that they are all informed of the activities of the project, at appropriate levels. Some stakeholders are enablers and some are a decision force. And where possible, try to get the stakeholder engaged in your project. See if they can champion a cause within the context of your project. Let each stakeholder feel and have ownership of a part of your project or portfolio. Let them identify, link, a part of their success with the success of your project. They will then help you, and themselves, succeed.

# An easy way to do Product Research

**PRODUCT RESEARCH IS LIKE A BACKGROUND CHECK FOR A NEW PRODUCT IDEA.**
*~ How to Do Product Research* **by Louise Balle**

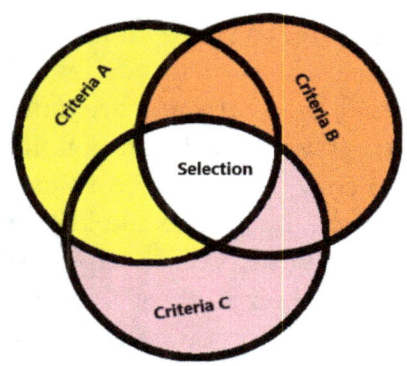

As a manager you will sooner or later need to do Product Research in order to select a Product or a Vendor for your projects, company, or a client.  I learned this technique when I needed to select a product for our client's needs.  And the market was full of promising products.

The first thing I did was to create a list of the key requirements the product needed to meet and satisfy.  Then I searched the Internet for products, which met the criteria.

I then presented these findings to my client to get their buy-in, up to that point.  It is always best to keep the stakeholders involved and have them feel involved and take ownership (up to a point).

I then called up the vendors and arranged for them to individually conduct presentations for our engineers, the client team, and myself. I told them that we will be considering other vendors as well.

During the individual, and separately held presentations by each of the vendors, I asked some basic questions:

1. In your view -who is your strongest competitor?
2. How are you better than them?
3. What is their weak point?
4. Why should we consider your product?
5. Why should we consider you?
6. How robust is your product?
7. What is your product warranty?
8. What kind of support do you provide?
9. Do you include any training?
10. For Department of Defense (DoD) contracts – can your product/services (if IT related) be procured through  Computer Hardware, Enterprise Software and Solutions program (CHESS), which is a leading contracting vehicle for federal IT purchases and procurement, at the DoD.
11. Can you provide some discounts on your products?
12. Do you have a backlog of orders
13. Where needed, I also ask whether the vendor will be willing to demonstrate their product in the client's environment.

Etc., etc.…

Their response usually will point out the weakness of their individual competitor's product. Sometimes they will even point out the product-support differences. They may even offer incentives.

Once you have the list, weed out the vendors, and products that do not meet your requirements and call the remaining vendors individual to address specific weaknesses. Then again assess their answers.

Once you have a short list, and where possible, have the selected vendors demonstrate their product. Invite your client (remember your client is one of the stakeholders) to the demonstration put up by the vendor. This approach usually makes the vendors happy also since they get to tout their wars to the end user/recipient.

Many times, the client is your corporate office and the stakeholder is an internal one. The basic approach should be similar whether the client is internal or external.

**PRODUCT RESARCH TEAM**

Once you have a list of the final contenders, and you have evaluated all the points you can then, with input from your stakeholders, you can evaluate and determine which Vendor(s) or Product(s) will be best for your project. And proceed accordingly.

Why do I say 'Vendor(s) or Product(s)'? Sometimes you need more than one product to complete the solution. Besides, some products work well with other specific products. So, you may end up selecting a suite of products which work well together and they may be more compatible with each other and may compensate for some capabilities the other products do not have.

I have used this approach for many projects. This has included products with Virtualization capabilities, hardware products which have included desktops, servers, operating systems, networks, database systems, software products, and even vendor services.

During the selection process I have also negotiated and acquired training services from the vendors under consideration. And most importantly, installation support, Technical Support (during the teething process – or getting used to the new product, or integration of the product into an existing system).

Here is a hint: you will find that the salesforce of many vendors (in the Technology field), have access to the brightest, or most experienced, minds in the company. So, in order to get support from those people is invaluable. My staff had to provide such support when I was working for IBM. The salespeople would promise the prospective customer the IT Moon (so to speak), and my staff had to make that a reality. The salespeople would of course ask our opinion when the prospective client asked for a capability. But when we told the sales people that it would be pushing the technology envelope to provide that capability, they would in turn tell the prospective client that it could definitely be done. However, if we told the sales people that it would be impossible, then they would back down.

So, do tap into the vendor's sales team's Technical support to get your new acquisition integrated into your system.

# Staff Readiness

**IF YOU WAIT FOR THE MANGO FRUITS TO FALL, YOU'D BE WASTING YOUR TIME WHILE OTHERS ARE LEARNING HOW TO CLIMB THE TREE**
*~ Michael Bassey Johnson, Master of Maxims*

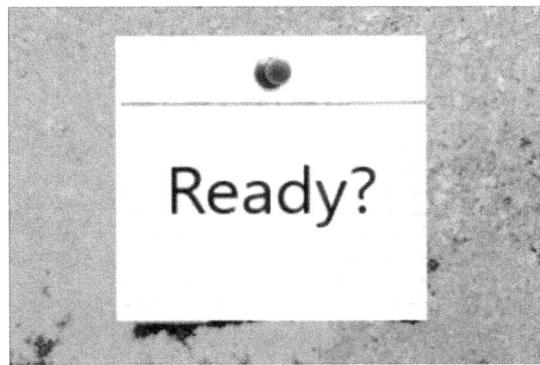

A project's chances to succeed will be greatly enhanced if the project staff are willing and able to complete the requisite tasks for the project. The schedule must be met and the cost has to remain within budget.

People are the key – so, is the project staff ready <u>and</u> qualified/trained to handle the project? What can you do if that is not the case? And what can you do to improve their effectiveness?

I found that one big motivating factor for people is one's desire to truly and genuinely help them – both in their personal lives and professional lives. Allow them to grow. Provide them opportunities to learn and grow in their chosen careers. Help others even in their personal lives, without getting tied into their personal affairs, where their personal matters intersect with the work (and it usually does).

I also found that often the client is interested in ensuring that the staff who works on their tasks are knowledgeable about the product and technology – after all it affects them. So, whenever our team wrote proposals for new business, we would include a training budget in the costs. And when time came, I discussed 'staff training' with the client (even if it was not already included in the contract – which can happen when one takes over an existing/ongoing contract).

Need for training can arise when one is acquiring or considering a new product. Or often when a product, currently in use, is updated/upgraded. And upgrades often happen when one is using industrial strength software products like Microsoft and Oracle (to name some). Or even when a new product line is introduced by a vendor. The same is also true for hardware products like networks, computers, etc.

Whenever we acquired a product, or discussed acquisition of a product or services from vendors I would bring up the question of training. I would ask vendors whether they would be willing to provide any training, without additional cost, if we were to recommend their product to the client. More often than not, the vendor would be willing to provide some training.

In one case, VMware was willing to provide training to developers and also to managers, in the setup and use of VMware software, which would also prepare the people who underwent training, a pre-prep towards VMware certifications.  You see this would work to the advantage of both – the developers and also VMware since with proper training there would, hopefully, be fewer help-desk/product-support calls and a certified VMware engineer/developer would increase the chances of commitment to use their products.

**READINESS**

In all training cases, I also set aside some seats for the client's personnel (technical and supervisory staff), in case they wanted to avail this opportunity for their staff.  This would also allow them to efficiently oversee the project deliveries, should they so choose to.  They would also become aware of the complexities of the product.

For my staff – this was an added incentive, since they were learning a new skill, or fortifying their knowledge of an existing skill. And I was not shy to point out that they could add the skill/certification to their resumes for future. So, it was win-win situation for all.

Our clients supported it whole heartedly, once they realized the cost saving in getting free training. And since we would include it in budgeted costs, we could always spend the money (wisely) on needed training, which was not product specific, or where a vendor was reluctant to provide 'no-cost' training.

The training contributed a lot to staff-readiness for us. I felt that we were prepared better to deal with issues, as they arose, since training always fills in cracks in 'product and functionality' knowledge.

# Blaze your path

**NO ONE SAVES US BUT OURSELVES. NO ONE CAN AND NO ONE MAY. WE OURSELVES MUST WALK THE PATH.**
*~ Gautama Buddha, Sayings of Buddha*

What do you believe in? How do you feel you should manage your projects? Only you can answer that. And you have to think it out, go through the steps of how you think the project(s) should progress. Who are the stakeholders, what is important to them?

There is the recommended classic way to handle the project (and there are many recommendations), however your way may be a blend of the classic principles. You have to answer that, but do not hesitate to experiment (within reality) your method of handling the project(s). Every project is unique, even when following the Standard Operating Principles (SOP) for managing a project. Just make sure that you have covered all bases and important issues.

One cannot be creative about deadlines and delivery dates. One can, however, be creative in blending one's own techniques with the classic approach on how one can achieve those objectives.

There may be a situation where switching resources could yield higher efficiency and time gains. This could be the result of a resource you are switching in, who may have a better grasp of the subject matter. Or you may even consider exchanging (temporarily) resources with another project based on your project's needs and their project needs.

Or you may consider sub-contracting or outsourcing a specific sub-task without affecting the budget. The sub-contractor may have done excellent work for your company in the past.

In all cases one will have to work within the framework of security needs and the infrastructure, policy, corporate culture constraints. Though the creative approach you apply would be entirely up to you.

We were planning deployment and rollout of Virtualized platforms for each state in the Continental US (CONUS) and all Outside the Continental US (OCONUS) location for the US Army. Unlike the first time when we did it, we had fewer Engineering resources this time.

As a result it was going to take longer than we had planned to do so. The client was not concerned since we had always managed to meet our planned and approved dates (these were only planned dates).

During a meeting to discuss this issue, the Chief Engineer suggested that since the Hotline Team had engineers we could explore that avenue.

I then went and discussed this with 3-4 Hotline Team engineers before discussing it with their manager, to make sure that they would be willing if their management approved.

This would have involved the individual engineers travelling to each site where the Virtualization platform was to be deployed. The process involved backing up the site's system, installing the new software, verifying it, starting it up, and turning it over to the site-engineer to verify operations and then backing it up again before making it go live. This entire process would take about 2 days with an additional day to spare, planned for contingencies.

The other advantage presented to the Hotline Team engineers was that my team would provide them training on all the tasks before they left. We mentioned the fact that they would have training, in-field experience, and that they would then have a leg-up on Hotline calls relating to issues related with Virtualizations.

After discussions with the Virtualization Provider/vendor we also arranged training to get Virtualization certifications. While we opened up training for our staff, we had told the Hotline Team engineers that they would get equal priority with our staff to get a training slot.

At the same time we also left two slots open for the customer in case they wanted to get their engineers or engineering managers trained in Virtualization Technology.
The customer was, as usual, happy and utilized this opportunity to get select staff trained. After all, people who supervise contractors (our team) also need to understand the systems they are going to supervise.

We gave the engineers the option of selecting the site (from a list) and selecting the date (again from a list – coordinated with the site staff). Once we got Hotline Manager's approval we finalized the plans (who – where – when). Some engineers took advantage of this opportunity to visit their home states also.

We completed all the tasks and the rollout with the help of the Hotline Team (their engineers were all-rounders and very knowledgeable), within our planned time and budget. The sites receiving the service and the upgrades were all very happy, as was the customer.

We got our tasks accomplished and the Hotline Team engineers also got the training and some also went ahead with obtaining their Virtualization Certification. Not only did they benefit, even our staff got some relief in the sense that the typical Hotline Desk calls to our engineers were dramatically reduced. The call volume to our engineers was reduced for support of newly deployed software and hardware, and also day-to-day support.

All this, since we trained and utilized the frontline staff for our deployment.

This is just one example of this type of approach. One should not feel limited or bound by the lack of resources or talent. Every company has talent and opportunities waiting to be explored if we are willing to extend ourselves beyond the seeming boundaries.

# Be Proactive

**RECAST YOUR CURRENT PROBLEMS INTO PROACTIVE
GOALS**
*~ Suze Orman*

Be as proactive as possible in all things you do. This will keep you ahead of the game. I have learned the hard way that your inner voice guides you. This learning, or lesson, came late in life for me. While I always tried to be proactive, and not postpone things, there were many times when a thought would arise in my mind that I should do such-and-such, and often I would tell myself 'Yeah I should do it' but I would not do it immediately.

When I did not follow the first dictate of an action-thought, it was usually late to do it right, later on. Then it was always trying to play catch-up, to handle the situation. This I wish I had learned early on. A lot of time and angst would have been saved.

This is where I realized that the sub-conscious mind is connected with everything.

The more we give the active mind an opportunity to connect with the sub-conscious at the mental level, and take heed of what it brings forth to the conscious level, the more we develop the ability to (sub-consciously and unconsciously) act at the right time.

The examples of this are peppered through my personal and professional life. It could be as simple as writing an email or a memo. Or to arrange a meeting with someone or group. Or keeping stakeholders abreast of the latest developments in their area of interest or sponsorship.

One has to be judicious in what one acts upon. Otherwise it could end up being 'impulsive'. Do not act on bad things, act only on the benevolent things.

So, how does one learn to discriminate? One way to determine what to act on was explained by a great spiritual Master.

He repeated the story of Lord Rama (from Indian Mythology) as stated in the Ramayana - Lord Rama was spending 14 years in a self-imposed exile in the forest, along with his wife Sita and younger brother Lakshmana.  One of His father's wives – Queen Kiekie wanted her son 'Bharat' to be king and asked her husband to send Lord Rama to the forest for 14 years, as a return-favor for the time when she had put her life in danger to save her husband's life.

One day, Ravana, the King of Shri Lanka, in the guise of a mendicant, abducted his wife Sita from their cottage in the forest.  He was smitten by her beauty and wanted to make her his queen.  Lord Rama and His brother Lakshmana later learned that Ravana had abducted her and organized an army and laid siege on Shri Lanka and rescued Sita.

As Ravana lay dying in the battlefield, struck down by Lord Rama's arrows, Lord Rama walked up to him and asked him – 'You have been a great devotee Lord Shiva (Hindu God) and a good King in the past, so what would your advice be to the common man?'  King Ravana said "You are the Lord and know it all, but since you have asked me let me say this in Sanskrit "Shubhashya Shigharam, Ashubhshya Kalaharam.  Meaning – when a good thought, a benevolent thought, arises in your mind – do it immediately, execute it immediately, but when a bad thought, a malevolent thought, arises in your mind – postpone the action as much as you can, since with passage of time good sense will prevail and you may give up (abandon) that bad thought/action".

He continued "Take my case –as a King I wanted to build a staircase to Heaven for my subjects, so they could ascend to the heavens.  But, I kept postponing it – I will do it after this…, I will do it after that…  And look at me now – I am dying and will leave this world without having built that staircase for my people".

Ravana went on "And a bad thought arose in my mind, blinded by lust, I abducted Noble Lady Sita, to make her my second queen.  I acted on an impulse – with the result that due to that ill-thought action, I lie here dying, shot down by your arrows. And therefore my advice to others is "Shubhashya Shigharam, Ashubhshya Kalaharam".

# Collaborate

COMING TOGETHER IS A BEGINNING, STAYING TOGETHER
IS PROGRESS, AND WORKING TOGETHER IS SUCCESS.
~ *Henry Ford*

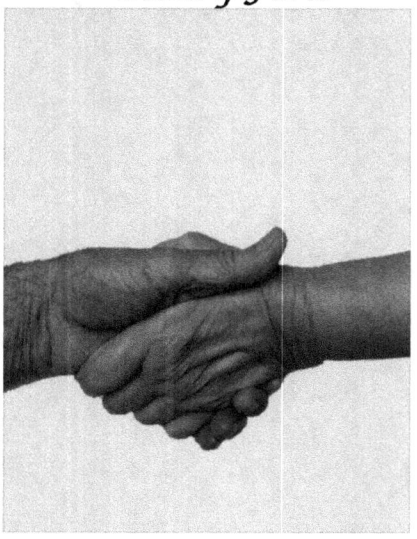

Develop a collaborative approach. There is strength and focused effort when we collaborate. One has to collaborate with all stakeholders. And stakeholders can be primary and tertiary.

I approached the most critical person on my client's team, who was the Technical Lead of the Security. She oversaw all the projects for our client. I told her that I wanted her to take a special interest in this particular project, which handled Personally Identifiable Information (PII) of all personnel. I requested her to help us make it most secure and to ensure that we are following all the Security Guidelines laid out by the government and her department, and to suggest remedial action where we are failing.

Her first reaction was that of surprise. No contractor in the past had approached her and sought her help and involvement. In the past, all the contractors had given her a wide berth and avoided getting her involved, till the last minute, since they considered Security to be a nuisance. A nuisance one had to deal with. A nuisance which was a part of their daily technical project work.

I also told her that I would send her drafts of our technical approach to the security issues and make her a part of regular reviewers so she can, if she had time and inclination to, review our other technical briefs, project reports (at management level). She could alert us if we were missing the security aspect in our approach.

She was very happy to be a part of it. After all she was not only being elevated in importance but also recognized as a valuable part of the entire project. She was getting a platform for expressing her authority (read as Technical Authority) in a public forum.

She became a valuable ally over time. She also had good people working for her on the client side and we mutually benefitted from this collaborative relationship.

I later dedicated a separate section in my presentations for her Subject Matter Expertise (SME) and would invite her to put a slide in our presentations. This gave her a buy-in and ownership of our projects. A symbiotic relationship indeed.

We find such (symbiotic relationship) collaboration in nature as well: The crocodile opens its mouth and allows the Plover bird to enter its mouth to clean its teeth from time to time. The crocodile does not eat the bird, but the bird gets a free meal as it cleans the meat morsels out of the Crocodile's teeth. A Red Billed Oxpecker removes ticks from the ear of an impala.

Another example is that of the Galapagos giant tortoise and the finches (a bird) of Galapagos, including some mockingbirds. The birds fly in front of the tortoise to show that they are present. When and if the tortoise needs them then it stretches out its neck and legs so that the birds can reach ticks (and other parasites) which are often found on the skin of the tortoise. The Galapagos giant tortoise is thus rid of the parasites and the birds, in turn, get an easy meal. This is mutualism and collaboration.

**C O L L A B O R A T I O N - THE CROCODILE AND THE PLOVER BIRD**

We have to take lessons from nature, in symbiosis, mutualism, and collaboration. We can then leverage off each other's skills and knowledge to benefit mutually.

# Undivided Attention

**THE GREATEST GIFT YOU CAN GIVE ANYONE IS YOUR
UNDIVIDED ATTENTION**
*~ Will Schwalbe*

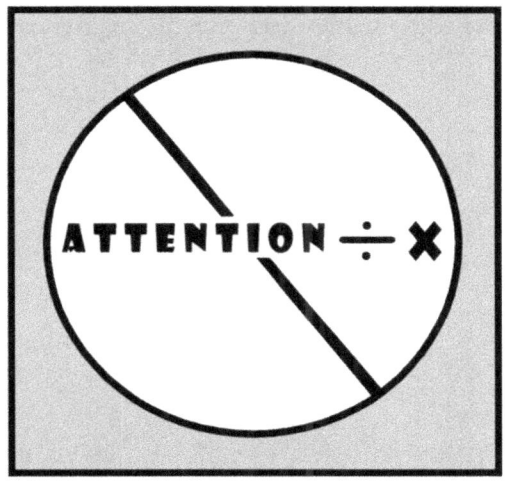

I had mentioned about Marv, who gave his full attention to anyone who walked into his office, similarly giving full attention to the task at hand always yields faster results.

This is like a student giving his/her full attention to the subject he/she is studying. Or when one is in a meeting and one pays full attention to the matter being discussed. Which means turning your cell phone off or to mute, so as not to be disturbed during the meeting.

Paying undivided attention expedites understanding and execution of tasks. One should concentrate on the task at hand so one can execute or dispose it off efficiently. This may avoid going back to it.

I found that my concentration was at its peak mid-morning. So, I would tackle complex tasks, difficult interviews, or complex presentations at that time. I would mute my cell phone if I was in such a meeting. Often I did not have the luxury of choosing my time, so then I had to make do with what I had.

Concentration and undivided attention helped me finish my tasks faster and with more care, avoiding many mistakes.

# Study Successful people

**BEHIND EVERY SUCCESSFUL MAN THERE'S A LOT OF UNSUCCESSFUL YEARS**
*~ Bob Brown*

**I HAVE NOT FAILED. I'VE JUST FOUND 10,000 WAYS THAT WON'T WORK**
*~ Thomas A. Edison*

**Study Successful people**

Observe and study the habits and traits of successful people around you and in your daily life. Try to cultivate those traits in yourself. Endeavor to emulate those traits.

We have done this all of our lives, as we were growing up. This is what often makes people go to the Gym. Sometimes we set an image of ourselves in our mind as a successful person and then we try to mold our lives accordingly.

One can learn to be successful by picking some trait from one person and another trait from another person. After all none of us is perfect.

I would sometimes go to people and tell them what I admire about them and that I would like to cultivate that very trait in myself. People have liked that and taken pains to help me move in that direction. Everyone likes genuine appreciation and they will go out of the way to help you achieve your goals.

Here are some examples of the traits of others I have tried to, or would like to, adopt myself:

- Mark is an excellent orator. He is sharp and a senior manager, who has the skill to get into the nitty-gritty of issues, and a part of his mind also views at a management level. He is also a shrewd planner and is able to chart his course to negotiate office politics to his advantage. What helps him in that is the fact that he is a good judge of people. He migrated from a technical career to a management career.

  I have tried to cultivate his qualities for myself, but where I willingly fail is negotiating Office Politics. I am just not built that way. I have had a past experience into simple politics and it left a bitter taste behind, so I try to avoid it. Let me share my past experience –

  > I was a student in my engineering college and studying for my Bachelors in Electrical Engineering. Since I was interested in book-reading, in my third year of college (it was a 5-year course) I decided to run for the seat of the Cultural Secretary for the year. Amongst other issues, the Cultural Secretary was also responsible for books in the college library, arts, etc.

  > A close friend of mine was interested in the seat for Deputy Cultural Secretary. So, we teamed up and opted to run as a team.

There were two other contending teams of "Cultural Secretary – Deputy Cultural Secretary". As time passed and we got closer to voting date, one of the teams dropped out, so we were two teams vying for the same slots.

One day I was approached by the Deputy Cultural Secretary hopeful for the other team and he told me that his supporters would vote for me and not his chosen-on-paper Cultural Secretary team member, provided my supporters would vote for him and not my own chosen-on-paper Deputy Cultural Secretary.

I was shocked at such a proposal. I told him I will not betray my running mate, and asked how he could even suggest such a thing. He told me that he had also never thought of betraying his running mate but found out about the underhand pact between my running mate and his running mate, that their supporters would secretly cross-support each other. I was in disbelief, or possibly denial, that people would be disloyal to each other over such a minor position.

Well – I did lose the election and it was won by my running mate as the Deputy Cultural Secretary, and my opponent as the Cultural Secretary. At that time I decided that I would never dabble in politics again, if people were disloyal over even such petty positions, what would happen when the stakes were higher? I have been happier since. I have had opportunities to dabble in politics but I have declined to get involved.

- Tom has been on the client side. An example of technical brilliance and a shrewd and capable manager. He puts on his Technical Hat when he is dealing with technical issues.

And since he understands technology, he has a quick grasp of issues, and what is involved in resolving them. He steers the project, keeping in mind the future of technology and the industry.

He puts on his Management Hat when he is executing management tasks. He usually has his management hat on all the time. And he has proved to be a very competent manager.

Above all – his most endearing quality is that he is a good human being. He is compassionate, not only to his staff, but also to his contractors.

- Bryan was also on the client side. A self-deprecating man, he understood technology and could explain complex issues with simple diagrams, charts, and figures. He worked very collaboratively. He was dedicated and sincere in his outlook. If he undertook something, he gave it his best and he always completed his tasks on time.

**SUCCESSFUL PEOPLE
( AND THEIR HABITS )**

There are many more examples. I have named just a few here. I have provided a list towards the end of this book on the winning (in my mind) traits various people have and something to learn from them. Every Person has qualities, we just have to identify them and try to cultivate them in ourselves.

# Give Credit where Credit is due

**NO MAN WILL MAKE A GREAT LEADER WHO WANTS TO DO IT ALL HIMSELF OR GET ALL THE CREDIT FOR DOING IT.**
*~ Andrew Carnegie*

Never take credit for the work, information, or accomplishments of others. Firstly, it is unfair. Secondly, you will lose credibility over time. Thirdly, you would not want others to take credit for your achievements either – so 'do unto others, as thou would have others do unto you'. This also undermines the confidence and trust in each other and in the team.

I have come across many instance where due credit was denied others. Here is an example - there was a newly promoted manager in our office. She was an excellent team player who constantly promoted her co-workers. However once she became a manager her personality underwent a radical change. She would take credit for the work, ideas, and efforts of her staff. Very quickly she lost the good will of the people who worked on her team. She underwent a complete transformation and neither her staff, nor her colleagues, appreciated that change. She was, however, oblivious to that. And it was to her detriment.

The team lost its cohesion and focus. Her staff was constantly trying to counteract her moves, instead of spending energy doing productive and creative activities in support of the project. As a result her team and the project suffered a downturn in productivity.

" Your son got an 'F' grade because he copied it from the Internet. Let us 'GIVE CREDIT WHER CREDIT IS DUE'. The Internet gets an 'A' grade."

Taking credit for other people's work is also plagiarism. It does not yield any benefit long term and undermines the credibility of the person.

On the other hand, giving credit to people for their contributions and achievements bolsters wellbeing in them and also boosts productivity. When people are recognized for their efforts, they want to contribute more.

Giving credit where it is due, should also translate into rewards, monetary or non-monetary, for the contributor. This encourages them further. And when people are recognized for their contributions, they endeavor to work harder and not hold back their creativity.

This approach also bolsters team morale. It creates an environment which is charged with good will and teamwork.

This was evident on one of my projects. Not only were the contributors appreciated and rewarded for their contributions by me, but I recognized their efforts in meetings with other groups and I reported their efforts to upper management. One of my staff members also proposed a system where co-workers could give a programmatic thumbs-up to their colleagues for any contribution which made the life of others easier. All these kudos were taken into considerations when the annual review time came.

An appreciated person is a happier, better, and willing participant towards the common goal.

# Let your Imagination take flight

**OLD WAYS WILL NOT OPEN NEW DOORS**
*~ Unknown*

Follow the beaten path by all means, but do not let that stifle your creativity. When you think that you have a unique approach to doing things, do not hesitate to put that to a test. Test your approach on a smaller scale, on a smaller task, or sub-task to verify that it works.

It may be a management process, procedure, or a product. Take it for a test-flight. And encourage your staff also to come up with suggestions to 'improve things' or to 'make them better'. Encourage them to come up with new ways and/or experiences of other companies to your projects. Discuss these ideas and the issues they will address, with all the stakeholders to get their opinion and buy-ins.

It is collaboratively and collectively that one can come with ways to improve solution handling.

This is how various new approaches in the field of Management, Business, Information Technology, Medicine, etc. were introduced, tried, and with success -became mainstream.

So, do not hesitate to let your imagination take flight and some of your ideas may become the success you desire and become your own approach and style.

All new ideas, inventions, methodologies, or concepts were something that someone thought of. Something that someone dreamed. And then worked to make them a reality. They took risks of failure, not once but many times, till they succeeded.

Thomas Edison's words should inspire us – he said "I have not failed. I've just found 10,000 ways that won't work. "

# Watch out for the Gatekeepers

**BOTH WOMEN AND COMPUTER SCIENCE ARE THE LOSERS WHEN A GEEKY STEREOTYPE SERVES AS AN UNNECESSARY GATEKEEPER TO THE PROFESSION.**
*~ Cordelia Fine*

**THE GATEKEEPER**

I was interviewing for the position of the VP of technology with a Department of Defense Information Technology contracting company. It was a small company with about 100 or so employees. The person interviewing me was the owner, and the President, of the company. There were two other people helping the President. One was the admin, and she was busy taking notes, the other person was a new graduate, and she was introduced as an intern. Which was kind of surprising to me since this was an interview for a senior corporate level position. But I thought maybe as part of her internship training she was shadowing the President, or maybe she was training for a Human Resources position.

Anyway, the interview went well. The President indicated that I was offering a unique perspective and approach for the position. And that he liked it. He also gave me his personal phone and email. I too had liked the guy. I left their office on a good note.

I later sent him a thank you note. Surprisingly - the response I received was from the intern. A couple of other emails back and forth made me wonder as to what the intern's role was. The President did respond once or twice, but it was mostly the intern. And she would take a couple of days to respond.

My pre-interview research of the company followed by my discussions with the President made me realize that the company could increase and expand their market penetration of the DoD market by utilizing Results from Data Analytics. I then developed a high level presentation for the President in order to show him positive and simple ways to improve their odds for winning new contracts and for expanding their potential client base. I even provided in my presentation some analytics results for them to use, even if they were not willing to hire me.

I wrote to the President, offering to do a presentation and provide the information for him to use. Not only did I want to share the information with him, but my primary motive was also to improve my chances of securing the position.

The President responded quickly to express interest. But again I was surprised by a response from the intern also, stating that it would not be fair to the other candidates if only I was given that opportunity, and not them. The president did not respond either to her note or me.

That was the turning point and I felt that it would not be a good idea to join this company since I may not have direct access to the president. I also felt that this intern exercised quite a bit of influence on the president and that the functional authority of the position I was vying for would be compromised to the extent that the position holder would not be able to execute his/her responsibilities appropriately.

I let the position go and did not correspond with the company further.

So, be wary of the Gatekeepers. When you come across one, assess the overall situation. Determine who much influence, or power, the Gatekeepers has. Is it beneficial to pursue your track further? Would you have cater to the Gatekeeper? Will it waste your time and resources in the execution of your duties? Then you can make a sounder decision whether to move forward.

# Be Wary of some of your Peers - All of them are Not Your well-wishers

**DON'T WORRY ABOUT THE PEOPLE WHO AREN'T HAPPY FOR YOU – THEY PROBABLY AREN'T HAPPY FOR THEMSELVES EITHER**
*~ quoteshumor.com*

There was a Project Lead in my office, with a different department, who was always competing with me. What I had, he seemed to want.

Since I had my own office and he shared his office with another person, he persuaded the Corporate Management that he needed a separate office. When I got a round table for my office, for meetings with my clients, he got one shortly after that. When I got a cabinet with locks, he got one too.

While I was amused at that, I did sense a lingering sense of jealousy, whenever I had to deal with him for his group's activities. I paid no attention to him and went about my project work. I heard later that he would go and complain about our project and would try to minimize the achievements of our team, to our client. He would instigate another department, where he had some close friends, to complain about me etc.

When our company lost the Federal contract to a competitor, as is usually the case when a contractor wins a contract for the first time, they approach the key people of the losing company, to hire them. I was also approached and offered a position with the winning company.

The recruiting manager was very respectful and pleased that I had accepted to interview with them. They had heard about me. I met with them and the next meeting was arranged with a senior corporate officer, the following weeks. The recruiting manager also told me the people they were going to interview soon, including the Project Lead who was jealous of me.

I suspected that after they interview that Project Lead, I may not hear from this company. And that is what happened, after a twist. They called me and wanted to know the projects under me and how I was handling them, including the Technical Details and my contacts with the client. I gave them some information but also told them that they would come to know the details, once I was a part of their team.

They did not call me again, except to postpone the meeting with the senior corporate officer. I felt that it was as well – I did not need to join then and get involved in their office games/politics. I had other opportunities in the works.

I heard later that the hiring company had that Project Lead join them, but let him go after two months. I do not know why. I also heard that they let a lot of newly-hired senior staff go. I was glad I had not joined that company.

This is just one of many examples. I am sure that a lot of others have had experiences with peers, who are jealous of them. We should not brood or worry about such people. We should go on doing our work, just be wary of such people and keep them at a pleasant arm's length from us and our team.

Another example is at a different company. Our client was very vocal and they would appreciate or criticize, in a general meeting our (contractor's) staff depending on what they were expecting and what they got.

I would often receive open appreciation from the client for our team's work. The manager of one of the other development groups seemed not to like that praise, directed towards our team.

She would often take an opportunity, to go behind the back of our corporate officers, and talk to the client criticizing me and our team. I did not know how to block that, so I would just continue working, as I had always done. I would concentrate on my work, and would not make any comment, even when I was told by the client of this behavior. I would just tell the client team that our work was a proof of our dedication to the project. The products we deployed for our client were the ones with the least amounts of defects during testing.

And our products, when they went to deployment did not have any defects, they were on time and very well documented. We also gladly provided training to our client's clients/customers/users. And in turn, that group were happy with the products they got, and the follow-on support they got from our team.

I had read in a book written by Dr. Robert Schuller, titled "Be an Extraordinary Person in an Ordinary World", that someone had asked him a question like – 'Reverend, how do I deal with people who try to put me down and always complain about me?' I remember Dr. Schuler replying 'When the Moon is full, in the sky, dogs come out and start howling. The Moon does not care. It keeps on shining. And you should keep on shining as well.'

I have learnt from his advice and always concentrate on my work and continue to try and 'shine'. While jealousy bothers me first, it then has always propelled me to do better work, so that my work speaks for itself and the unfounded and negative comments do not have a leg to stand on.

**THE MOON KEEPS ON SHINING WHILE THE DOGS HOWL**

The Spiritual Master has said – 'When someone criticizes you, examine yourself and the allegations. Should there be even one percent of truth in it, make amends and also ask for immediate forgiveness'. I take this to heart and try my utmost to live by it.

There is another example – Heather was a software developer for a small company. She had a lot of confidence in her capabilities. As she looked at her peers and seniors, she felt that she was capable of handling their jobs as well, if not better, than them. Yes she would need some familiarization with her job content, but it was no big deal and she could pick it up on the job.

One day that CEO of the company resigned. She felt that she had an opportunity to move up and she decided to approach the senior most person in the company, the decision maker, the President of the company. She then made an appointment to talk to him confidentially.

When she met him, she presented her interest in the position of the CEO. She cited her achievements, her drive and her capabilities. She said she was confident that she could handle the job.

The President knew her as a rising star and had confidence she could handle it in time. He was not sure of the timing though. Heather continued talking to him and he finally agreed. However, he told her that he would send her for some training, but cautioned her to keep this to herself and to not let those around her. Particularly her immediate boss.

Heather kept it to herself. She went to, and completed, her training and on her return, she assumed the position of the CEO for the company. There was resistance in the people around her initially. They felt that she had not paid her dues, and she needed to rise slowly through the ranks. She, however, was confident that she was ready and had reached a point in her career to take the lead. And she did.

**ANY "FRIEND" WHO ISN'T HAPPY WHEN YOU ARE HAPPY IS AN ENEMY WHO HAS INFILTRATED YOUR CAMP?**
*~ Rigel J Dawson*

In his second book, "Looking Out For #1" (a *New York Times* best seller), Robert Ringer has developed the Leapfrog Theory 'Leapfrog Theory: In business, you are under no obligation to fight your way up "through the ranks" or let someone else decide when you've "paid your dues." Only you know when you're ready, and when you are, leapfrog to exactly the point on the business ladder where you think you belong'.

Robert Ringer was also the author of the bestselling book (his first book) 'Winning through Intimidation'. His life shows that he was a man who did not give up easily. This bestseller was rejected 23 times. He finally self-published the book and it became a bestseller and was on the Best Seller list for 36 weeks.

So, have confidence in yourself. Do not be intimidated by your peers, or those around you, in believing (what they will have you believe) that you are not ready, or that you have to pay your dues before you can rise. No one knows, better than you, how capable you are.

# Office Bully

**COURAGE IS FIRE, AND BULLYING IS SMOKE.**
*~ Benjamin Disraeli*

**NEVER BE BULLIED INTO SILENCE. NEVER
ALLOW YOURSELF TO BE MADE A VICTIM.
ACCEPT NO ONE'S DEFINITION OF YOUR LIFE,
BUT DEFINE YOURSELF.**
*~ Tim Fields*

**BULLIES ARE COWARDS AT HEART**

It was my first consulting assignment. The Company I worked at had a Deputy PM who was strongly built and mean looking. He had a habit of bullying consultants. He would often tell them that he would slap them till they got it right and he would slap them if they did not beat the schedule by at least a day.

This behavior always surprised me, more so since the other consultants kept mum. They did not oppose his behavior. They were probably afraid of being fired from their consulting jobs.

One day this Deputy PM turned on me and started saying that I should take it as a warning that he would slap me, etc. I immediately got angry with him and told him "I will kick you till you are sore and then slap you some, unless you want to be friends and this is a joke". He was taken aback and kept quiet. Thereafter he always spoke respectfully with me. I had not only called his bluff, but stood my ground.

Bullies usually are overbearing and throw their weight around, but they are cowards at heart. And when challenged legitimately, they back down. Some do turn vicious, but if you continue to show courage, to take them to task, they will give up. They will behave.

Bullies are also sheep in a wolf's clothing. They appear tough initially. And their mannerism and behavior support the appearance of a tough person. Many bullies have continued to bully others since they have never been challenged before. However, once confronted, they often back down and do not repeat that offence.

Many times people are afraid, not of the bully, but of other consequences. In an office environment, people maybe fearful of losing their jobs. Particularly if the bully's behavior seems to be sanctioned by upper management or a specific manager. For myself, I have not been afraid to challenge a bully's behavior, because if you allow the behavior once, it will perpetuate and continue. In my opinion, one has to nip it in the bud.

I am not saying that you should always challenge a bully, but you have to defend yourself. And you have to assess your situation and the risks involved. And once you challenge a bully then you will have more confidence the next time. Your reputation will also grow.

There was another incident in another office. A Senior VP was holding a department meeting and I was attending it also. Someone took the opportunity to complain about my project team's lack of cooperation with their team and said that I was not helping them meet their schedule.

Since I, and my team, were the target of the complaint, incorrectly in my opinion, I started to explain, but the Senior VP tried to hush me up. He said " A...A...A...". He would cut me off every time I spoke. I was not cowed down by this behavior. He even started saying "LaLaLa...I cannot hear youuu...LaLaLa..." However, I continued to talk, saying "You have to hear both sides, you cannot just Sh...Sh...Sh..., me or the issue. Since it has been brought up and the complaint has been made to you, I have to bring out the facts, and since everyone is here the truth will come out, etc. etc.

There was another VP who was going to take over this Senior VPs portfolio in 6-7 months. He realized that there probably was more to this issue and he turned to the Senior VP and said they should let me explain the issue. And I was able to explain the issue without any more interruptions. The result was that the matter was cleared in the favor of my team.

In the process, I also earned a reputation for not be being squeamish about challenging authority, if they were incorrect. And the incoming VP also observed that.

After the incoming VP assumed the daily responsibilities of the portfolio, we kept a pleasant relationship. He was very sharp and astute – whenever he had a touchy subject to discuss with me, and if it was in the public Project domain, he would have a team of people with him. He would call me on the phone and ask me if I had time to step into his office. The first time I was surprised that he had a team of people with him, since he had not mentioned it, but I got used to his approaches.

**A Bully is a 'SHEEP' in a FOXE'S clothing**

Furthermore, in order to avoid becoming a victim of bullying, by my seniors (in rank), I used to let them know, at the first opportunity that they were managing the tasks/projects I was working on. They were NOT my bosses. I would say something like "I respect the position you hold, that of managing the projects I am working on. I adhere to the chain-of-corporate-command, but my Boss is the One Upstairs. No one other than 'He', is my Boss".

I would also tell my staff, if they ever called me their boss that I was basically supervising and managing the tasks they were working on. That I was not their boss, and that 'He' upstairs was the actual boss. I lived by the code that I preached.

# Do not throw anyone under the bus

**GOOD LEADERSHIP ISN'T ABOUT ADVANCING YOURSELF. IT'S ABOUT ADVANCING YOUR TEAM.**
*~ John C. Maxwell*

The Company I worked for had a common work practice - all senior staff had to do a presentation every week to upper management and another one to the client counterpart. We presented our progress, as well as, brought up any problems, issues, plans, or focus areas.

And that we had to do presentations every month to larger audiences - which included all client members and all the managers and senior engineers and architects or the partnering companies. And those were the days of transparencies. Those were the days before PowerPoint.

We got into the habit of whipping up presentations quickly, and also developed comfort and ease of doing presentations in front of crowds. And as our project development and deliveries grew, so did the presentation complexities and attendance (number of people).

Prior to our presentations for upper management and our clients we often did a dry run. The manager on my project would often be my first audience. That manager would, more often than not, ask for changes in the slides. Even though I would not agree, I would comply. After all she was the manager and this was her project. Later when I would do the presentation to our upper management, and they would ask why it was this way and not the way (I had originally constructed the slide) this manger would say ' Yes Vikram, why is it this way, it should actually be the other way' (which is how I had it originally, before she had asked me to changed it).

This would totally throw me off. After all, it was she who had asked me to change it in the first place, and now she was putting me down, instead of admitting it was her suggestion. She was throwing me under the bus and making it look as though it was my error, lack of understanding, etc. I was taken aback the first two-three times and kept quiet. But this continued, so I would respond with - 'Why, you are the one who had me change it this way, I had it the correct way to begin with'.

This time the manager was taken aback, and she stopped for

a short while. Then again resumed this. And when I protested, she would say - 'No, that is what I said, but you obviously misunderstood me'.

So, I had to switch to plan B - I went and talked to the equivalent of the Program Manager, who was the manager's manager. I asked him whether I could run my draft presentations by him, vial email, first. He would get a preview, as well as it would save him, and me, overall time. Since I could address any questions he had ahead of time and would incorporate them in the final presentation to him. He said 'I understand what you are trying to do here - so okay'. Since he seemed to understand my real reasons, I said 'Allow me to send the draft presentations to you alone, for a couple of times, then I will start including the manager as well, later on'. He agreed.

The results were as expected. The Program Manager understood what was happening. He realized what the manager was trying to do. And Later I made it a habit to send a draft to both of them. This also prevented the manager from undercutting me.

The Program Manager must have had a discussion with the manager since her attitude towards me changed and she became aloof. So, I decide it was time to move on to the other side of the project/program.

I approached the Systems Engineering manager and asked him whether he would consider me for a Systems Architect/Engineer position, when one became available. As it is, I had always been interested in the Systems Engineering side of the project, rather than the software side. He said he would. I kept in touch with him. I would also send him new magazine articles on engineering. He was a bold and creative manager. He took an interest in my skills and enthusiasm.  And finally, after six months, he created a Systems Architect position in his group and transferred me into his group, with the blessings of the Program Manager.

While I would not have behaved the way this manager behaved with me, I decided even more firmly to never put any one else in a similar situation.

Do not throw people under the bus even if they have committed an error.  We are all humans and make mistakes.  However if someone is willfully negligent in performing their tasks then be strict with them.  Look at the history - if the person is not habitually in error then work them to rectify the situation.

On the other hand if the person is habitually in error, but is sincere, then see if you can salvage their situation where you can assign them to handle things where they are less likely to commit errors.

Besides the people factor, you also owe your stakeholders (clients, upper management, other staff, etc.) their due, so if someone is not performing at their optimal to meet the strategic goals then you need to take decisive action to separate them from the situation temporarily or worse - permanently.

CD, the developer mentioned elsewhere in this book, had a task completion on the critical path, and was late on the delivery of a sub-task. I viewed the project schedule, and noted that there was some redemption if she fast-tracked on the next sub-task.

This issue came up in our next "cross-project, program-schedule" meeting. Now a lot of managers turn to their developers to take the heat at such a time. I did not follow that track.

As other Project Managers enjoyed our missed sub-task schedule delivery. They were enjoying it because our project was usually ahead of the curve and we had not missed any schedule tasks so far. For this reason our client was very happy with our project team. Here was a chance for other projects to give us a black eye, and cast us in poor light.

They complained, moaned, said their scheduled would be affected. I took the heat for the missed deadline, and told all project managers/leads that we had a recovery plan. Which I shared with them.

We did deliver on time and the day was saved.

# Respect People

**PEOPLE WILL FORGET WHAT YOU SAID, PEOPLE WILL FORGET WHAT YOU DID, BUT PEOPLE WILL NEVER FORGET HOW YOU MADE THEM FEEL.**
*~ Maya Angelou*

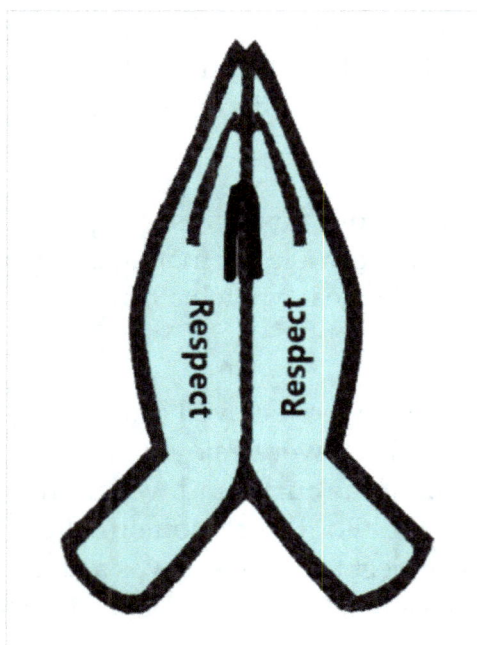

When I was about 14-15 years old, I and my friends had formed a band. The band practiced in the verandah (sort of a covered porch) of one member. We were excited since two of the band members had talent. One played the guitar (and he played it well, in our opinion), and the other was (Drum roll please.......) a drummer. The other three, including myself, made a lot of noise and could belt out a few songs. It was the Beetles, Elvis, Nat King Cole, and Cliff Richard era.

We met and practiced a minimum of 3-4 times a week. Some weeks we managed to meet 6-7 times. We had great expectations from ourselves. And we were going to be famous. After all, a lot of the bands had started in garages.

After a few months we felt that we needed some female voices to join the band (and it would be great way to meet girls too), so we invited some girls, who we felt could sing, from our schools and neighborhood, to come and meet with us.

I remember that first meeting well. After our discussions and some practice songs were over, and it was time to go home. I was the first one to walk out the door. One of my band members showed finesse and stepped aside letting the girls walk through the door before him. And the first girl to step through the door remarked loudly 'Ram is such a gentleman, unlike some others', looking pointedly at me.

I was embarrassed, to say the least, and I had not even thought of it. But that lesson has stayed with me till today. Be polite, be thoughtful of others, and in all situations - be a Gentleman, be a Lady.

This applies to all human beings one deals with. One should be mindful in dealing with others. Be respectful of others. When you are respectful, people will deal with you respectfully in return.

This is even more important when you become a manager, a team lead, a team member, etc., since it applies not only to your staff, but to all stakeholders. Respect begets Respect.

It is even more important when you are dealing with people with an inimical attitude towards you. You will sometimes be pleasantly surprised by the other person's behavior towards you.

There was only one time when being a gentleman towards a lady, almost backfired on me. When I went from 'Driver's License test' in Washington DC. It had two parts, one was a written test - which I passed with flying colors (only because it was simple and I had been driving for many years in India). This was followed by a road test. The Motor Vehicle Employee asked me to point out my car and go and wait for her.

When she came over to the car to sit on the passenger side - I leaned over and opened the door for her (as a gentleman of course). She got visibly upset. Throughout the duration of the road test she was very curt and abrupt. I of course did not understand the reason for her behavior. She had cooled down and normalized by the end of the test. She told me that I had done well.

I then asked her whether she would answer a personal, but a general question. She said 'okay'. I asked her as to why she had gotten upset earlier. She told me that she had thought that I opened the door for her because I wanted some leniency on the test, but realized later that I probably did not need it, so she became normal. I told her that I had learned early in life to be a gentleman.

I realized later that while all people like to be treated respectfully some women do not want to be given special treatment as women. They want to be treated like their male counterparts in the work environment.

So, always be a gentleman, especially in a social environment, but be respectful, irrespective of the circumstances. Be even more mindful as you become a lead/manager.

People who work with you, or for you, all need respect, just like you would. When you become a manager, you have been given the responsibility to manage the tasks. And that includes time and talent of the resources you have available to you. You have not been given sovereignty over people.

I always reminded the managers I reported my tasks to, that they were not my bosses, my Boss was the almighty. They were managers of the tasks, projects, programs, etc., and the resources they were given, including my time and skills as they related to my projects, programs, etc. So, while I respected them, I did not bow to them. I was open about the skills they had and appreciated their skills and expertise (if they had any).

When the staff on my team called me 'boss', I reminded them that we all work together, and there is truly only one Boss - the Almighty.  I manage their resources as they relate to tasks and their completion.

As a manager you are given a responsibility you need to fulfill relating to your work and the resources provided to you.  So, you respect people, whether they work on your tasks or other tasks.

One should also respect people in business meetings and private meetings. When one does that one will see an uptick in the way the meeting unfolds and way people treat you back.

I have also learned that while we love our children, and we are strict when it comes to discipline and their behavior, if we are respectful to them as individual human beings, they develop a self-respect which is one of the keys to confidence and success in life.

# Talk the Talk and (*most importantly*) walk the Walk

### WHEN YOUR ACTIONS CONTRADICT WORDS....YOUR WORDS DON'T MEAN ANYTHING.
### ~ *Quentin McCall*

Talk the Talk and (most importantly) walk the Walk, or as some say 'Walk the Talk'. Do not give false promises or unrealistic hopes – that is falsehood and will be exposed in due course of time. After that you will not be trusted. This holds true for your staff, management, clients, friends and relatives.

Know and recognize the boundaries of your knowledge and capabilities, but do not forget the environment and the odds of accomplishment, before you promise something. When you do that, you will in due course come to be recognized as 'one who delivers'.

Do continue the process of learning everything you can, about the work, the needed skills, and the requisite knowledge.

Never underestimate your capabilities, and where there are gaps in your knowledge and capabilities about a particular aspect, do not hesitate to ask people's advice. Turn to those who are considered experts. People are often flattered when you ask them for their valuable advice. I have found that those people are more than willing to help and assist one, when one approached them humbly.

## EXPERTS ARE PEOPLE WHO HAVE MADE ALL THE MISTAKES THEY COULD, IN THE NARROW FIELD OF THEIR EXPERTISE.
### ~ Niels Bohr

I often found that the staff was more skillful, or knowledgeable, about a specific task, so I let them handle it. I made sure that the customer and the upper management were aware about the skill and knowledge of the staff. This encouraged them further to complete the task. I learned from them from a distance, so as not to get in their way.

As a manager, one has to recognize the adeptness of the staff and give them credit. This is an integral part of "Walking the Talk". One has to properly delegate and get the task accomplished. Or one has to learn (the expert could very well be in another department) from the experts and do it oneself.

I have even turned to the client, if he/she is knowledgeable, and the only one with that knowledge. And this is the only hope. This has worked out in favor of both – where the client is the final approving authority. Once they guide you, they are bound to approve it if it comes out with the right result.

# Follow your inner voice

**DON'T LET THE NOISE OF OTHERS' OPINIONS DROWN OUT
YOUR OWN INNER VOICE.**
*[Stanford University commencement speech, 2005]
~ Steve Jobs*

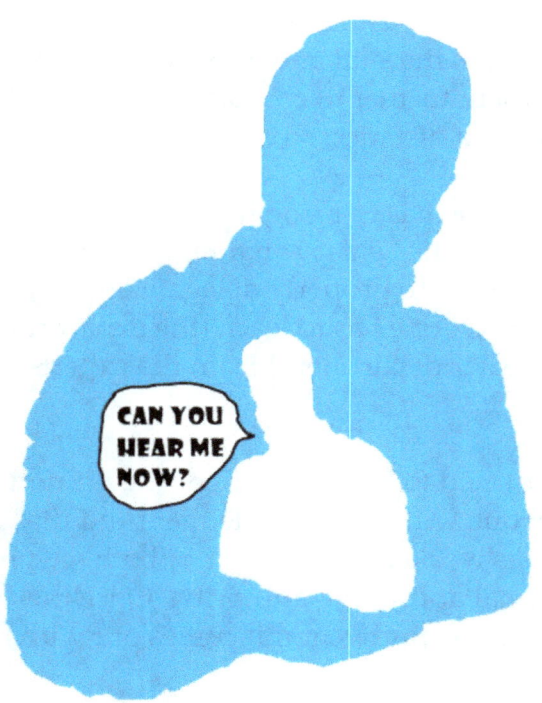

I often get a thought, an inspiration, or a suggestion from my inner self to do something. Like - take an action, perform a task now, send this email, do that activity. I have learnt to differentiate between a stray thought and my inner voice. All of us have the capability to hear that voice, which is unique to each one of us. We have to be willing and open to our sub-conscious thought process in order to hear it meaningfully.

I found that when I ignored such suggestions, from my inner self, I ended up trying to do damage-control later, rather than doing timely-action. Over time I have learned to identify and follow the dictates of my sub-conscious mind. This is how I learned to identify my inner voice and differentiate it from 'just a thought'. So, when I pay heed to my inner voice, and follow through with the recommended action, I am ahead of the ball game (so to say).

I have a lot of anecdotes to share on this topic. One simple example is that one day, just as I was about to leave the office for the day, I go an email from a Team Lead of another group, complaining about the lack of timely support from my team, resulting in delays in their delivery of a software module. The email was addressed to me with a CC to my Deputy PM, my Chief Engineer, and my Chief Architect. When people send out such emails, it is usually to put blame on someone else for one's own folly. I also did not know to whom else the email was Bcc'd (Blind Carbon Copied).

I was irritated by this email and I thought I will respond to it in the morning, but the inner voice told me to respond immediately. So I did. I responded with an open CC to also the Program Manager, along with a CC to the Task Lead's Manager. I cited notes, reviews, and prior communications (where they had stated in a Software Review that they will be late), proving that it was not my team, but their own team who was culpable. I concluded by offering the help of our team engineer and a software, to their team, in order to overcome their own delay.

This was as well, since within a minute I got a call from the Program Manager, who seemed to be aware of the earlier email to me (the Program Manager was very likely Bcc'd on the email to me). The Program Manager told me that he was not aware of the earlier open communication from the other team, during the Software Review, that they would be late. End of story.

This also ties in to an earlier chapter, where we talked about not procrastinating activities. The sooner I respond to my inner voice, the sooner matters work towards resolution, progress, or conclusion. I was able to sleep better that night with this behind me.

The other examples are more, or less, dramatic. The key point is that these things have worked for me. So much so, that those around me, particularly my team, had come to know my nature. And if I were to send an email to, or with a CC to someone, and then shortly thereafter happened to walk into that person's office, not for the purpose of discussing the email, but just happenstance. They would ask if it was related to the email I had sent earlier, and they would sometime get defensive that they did not get an opportunity to take action yet. From their perspective, I did not like to procrastinate. Which, looking at the positive side, was good for productivity.

Start listening to your inner voice. It will never misguide you. Your inner voice will never direct you to harm yourself or others, it is a benign guidance. It guides you for your welfare and for the welfare of others.

**HIS MASTER'S "INNER" VOICE**

Be open to your inner guidance. If you get bad thoughts, harmful thoughts, they should be immediately rejected, they are not inner guidance. Humanity is one, and the inner guidance is for the welfare of all.

# Speak the Truth

**SATYAMEVA JAYATE**
**(TRUTH ALONE TRIUMPHS)**

*~ From Mundaka Upanishad - mantra 3.1.6*
*~ It is also the national motto of India*

**"IF YOU ABIDE IN MY WORD, YOU ARE TRULY MY DISCIPLES,
AND YOU WILL KNOW THE TRUTH, AND THE TRUTH WILL
SET YOU FREE."**
*~ From the Bible - John 8:32*

Satyameva Jayate nantram
Satyena pantha vitato devayanha
Yena kramamtysayo hyaptakama
Yatra tat satyasya paramam nidhanam

Truth alone prevails, not falsehood.
By truth the path is laid out, The Way of the Gods,
On which seers, whose every desire is satisfied,
Proceed to the Highest Abode of the True.

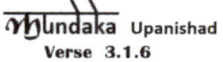

Mundaka Upanishad
Verse 3.1.6

## From the Mundaka Upanishad

When I was young, my father told me one day that he had
never spoken an untruth in his life. I did not believe that
statement since I thought it was not possible for anyone to
do that.

So, the next time I went to visit my paternal grandfather, during my summer vacation, I asked him about that statement. My grandfather confirmed it and said it was a fact – and that my father was a remarkable person. I then asked my father's sister also, and she too confirmed it. I then verified the same from my father's cousins and they too confirmed it.

On one of my visits home, after I had started working and had bought a separate house, my father mentioned that since he had always spoken the truth, now he had reached a stage that whatever he spoke, came true. He said "It happens. That is why I am afraid to speak of things, lest they actually happen."

I thought deeply about that statement and came to the conclusion that – either whatever my father says is fulfilled, or due to his truthful nature, he has reached a stage that he comes to know what will happen and thus what he says is fulfilled. In either case, that was the power of always speaking the truth.

I am not saying that my father was a saint, but he had that courage to speak only the truth. It takes moral courage to speak the truth. And it takes tremendous effort to always speak the truth. I also noticed that my father was bold and it could be because of this trait.

I have since tried to cultivate that in myself. We go through life, sometimes speaking white lies, which we think are harmless. Yet these traits sap our courage and weaken our integrity. They also weaken the words we speak.

The effect of, even attempting to speak the truth, has been a remarkable sense of strength. This is a very important trait for me, not in just my career, but also in my personal life.

When people realize that you have the habit of speaking the truth, they begin to trust you. I have always been upfront and truthful in my office and with my, or my company's, clients. And they have over time come to trust me and rely on me to give upfront answers. This sense of trust infuses into everyday life matters, both personal and related to business.

## SPEAK THE TRUTH - OR - YOU WILL HAVE TO COVER IT UP WITH MANY LIES

One can start speaking the truth by telling the truth to loved ones around oneself. After all, like Charity, Truth starts at home. For example, if you have a child, and the child asks you whether a medicine tastes nasty, or if an injection is going to hurt. Tell the child the truth, do not say a 'white lie'. Do not tone it down either. Be truthful, and encourage the child by telling him/her that the child is brave and can bear it. This will inculcate the habit of Truth in the child. The child will also grow-up trusting you and your words.

## A MAN SHOULD NOT SAY TO A CHILD, "I WILL GIVE YOU SOMETHING," AND THEN FAIL TO GIVE IT TO HIM, BECAUSE THIS WILL TEACH THE CHILD TO LIE.
### ~ The Talmud

Sometimes it is tough to tell the truth to one's spouse when faced with a question about finances – how are we doing? Or how much did it cost? Etc.  It is the same situation – try to start by telling the truth.  Or if one does not want to say it out, say something like "I do not want to tell", or "let us not discuss it".  At least this way you are not telling an untruth.

## A HALF-TRUTH IS THE MOST COWARDLY OF LIES.
### ~ Mark Twain

Sometimes people tell half a truth, or a partial truth.  That is even worse, since this is misleading.  It leads the other person to believe that what they are being told is the whole truth.  It is like speaking a truth.

Often it is very difficult to give an honest answer, at such times one can try to avoid saying anything.  The other person will get the right answer from your attitude.  It is better that they understand the truth than be misled into believing something which is not true and which will be detrimental to the situation.

One must have observed that when people do not speak the truth, they resort to untruths and continue to do so to cover up and give excuses. So much so that one starts disbelieving such people for all future actions.

I have heard people say something like 'Some of you have asked....' or that 'Some of you have suggested that...', do not say this unless it is the truth. Do not say it just to introduce, or to pre-dispose people to the acceptance of your ideas, if it is only your idea and 'some people...' have not said anything. This will dilute the strength of your words. They will not carry the weight of even a good idea. Endeavour to state the facts, and true facts.

It is important that your stakeholder trust you and the words you speak. They will believe you when you tell them that things are going well. They will believe you when you point out the serious consequences of following a particular track. They will trust your judgement and when you tell them bad news and also tell them that you will try to save the situation, or that things will improve due to such-and-such action you are taking, they will trust you and your judgement.

Truth leads to Trust.

# Adopt a Holistic Management Approach

**WE NEED TO MANAGE HOLISTICALLY, EMBRACING ALL OF OUR SCIENCE AND TRADITIONAL KNOWLEDGE - ALL SOURCES OF KNOWLEDGE. WE CAN DO THAT FROM THE HOUSEHOLD TO GOVERNMENT TO INTERNATIONAL RELATIONS.**
*~ Allan Savory*

A Holistic view is an all-encompassing, benign, and a complete attitude. A spiritual Guru once said that even if an Ant dies a premature death, the entire creation will become imbalanced. So, every aspect of this creation is important, every aspect of this universe is connected. Likewise, every aspect of the project is important. That is the approach we have to take, not only on life but in Project Management

According to the Savory Institute - Allan Savory developed Holistic Management, forty years ago. He proposed it as an approach to help land managers develop strategies for the regeneration of degraded landscapes and the livelihoods of the people living on them.

Today we can apply similar principles to Project Management. We have to view the Project not only as a temporary project as the PMI describes it [According to the PMBOK® Guide—Seventh Edition (ANSI/PMI 99-001-2021, p. 31)] the definition of a project is "a temporary endeavor undertaken to create a unique product, service, or result."

Projects are thus temporary and close down on the completion of the work they were chartered to deliver, but also having a legacy/lasting effect. Everything is connected and inter-connected. Everything we do, leaves a footprint on the fabric of time. Even long after the project is completed, however small, it leaves its impact on the people who were involved in it – the stakeholders, and also on the endeavor undertaken, and its related entities.

The ones who performed the tasks related to the project, add it to their experience. Similarly the management and the customer add it to their oversight experience. We all learn from that experience – if we do not, then we are not looking at the right place, we are, perhaps, not viewing it in the right perspective.

All of our Project needs, actions, and their results have a symbiotic relationship, whether it is Mutualistic or Commensalistic. As long as we keep that in mind and proceed forward we will benefit from our projects and at the same time help each other in our professional, and personal, journeys through life.

A holistic approach would be to keep everyone's wellbeing, welfare, and happiness in mind. To make project decisions, being mindful of the good of all, including the purpose of the project undertaking, is an attitude benevolence.

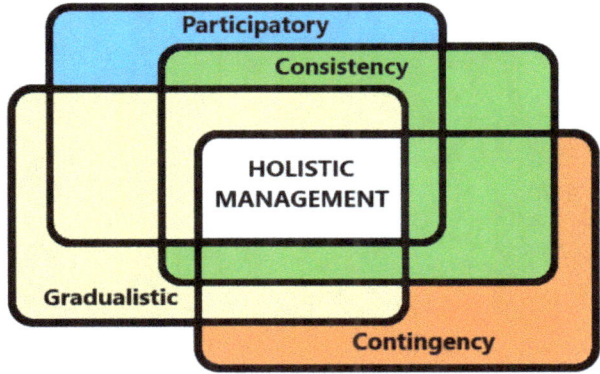

I have heard from two chefs that when cooking, if the cook is not happy, then the meal does not taste as good. One imbibes one's work with one's attitude and feelings. And this is not just from the manager's point of view but also from staff's, from the client's, and ultimately the project beneficiary's point of view also. So, this includes all the stakeholders, including the ones who will inherit the results of the project.

Our attitude should be benevolent, working for the good of all. Our approach should be such that everyone should benefit from the project, in one way or another. Either directly or indirectly.

Holistic is also Holographic. Wherein any part represents the whole. And 'whole' is reflected in every part. Remember 'What goes around, comes around'. Leave a legacy with every project that you attempt, and every project you complete.

# Acknowledge and Recognize

# people in public

**MY ANSWER IS: RECOGNIZE YOURSELF IN OTHERS.**
*~ Nadine Gordimer*

I was embarrassed that I could not remember the name of the one person who had told me his name the night before, (at a social gathering) and that he had connections in the company I was trying to get a job in. The next morning, try as I might, I could not remember his name. So, I saw this opportunity floating away.

Even though it was too late for this opportunity, I decided to do something about my 'poor' memory for names for the future. I always had trouble remembering names. So, I seriously did research in how to remember names. I found a technique that worked for me.

I then searched at home and pulled out my old copy of a classic book by Dale Carnegie - HOW TO WIN FRIENDS AND INFLUENCE PEOPLE. I felt I must re-read his book and adopt more principals in my daily and professional life. It would also refresh my memory since I had read this book a long time ago. After all his was the first mention, I had read about, about the importance of names. He had said "Remember that a person's name is to that person the sweetest and most important sound in any language".

So, I had to develop a technique to remember people's name. And after research I decided to make it a habit to repeat a person's name as often as circumstance would permit (and Dale Carnegie has also stressed this). So I started using a person's name in, conversation, as soon as I am introduced to a new person. I even have the person spell their name for me if I find it difficult. I try to anchor their name in my mind by some means – to the looks of the person, or the subject of the conversation . . . etc.

Dale Carnegie (by whom I was impressed and learnt a lot form whose book) cited the case of Jim Farley, who had little-to-no education, who became the Chairman of the Democratic Party and the Post Master General, had attributed his success, in an interview, to being able to recall ten thousand people's names. And corrected the interviewer on the number of people he could call by their first name was fifty thousand.

I still have difficulty with the few names I have to remember, but I keep working at it.

In the office I tried to wish everyone by their first name – from the President, to the Janitors and Cleaners (we are all humans doing our jobs with dignity). I would tell them my name, and ask for theirs. And memorize their names.

In my meetings I would go around and ask people for their name and greet them by their first name, if I knew it, including making a comment. I would also ask who all were dialed-in to the conference calls. I would write their names down. At the end of the meeting I would bring up the names of the people and note their comments down. Even people I had met only on the phone (they may be in another office, state, or country) were acknowledged by their name.

I followed this practice for all the people I dealt with, in person or remotely. And it appeared that people enjoyed communicating with me and attending my meetings.

I understood if someone did not want his/her presence acknowledged, and did not call out their name on the phone in a meeting. And I let it be.

After the meeting I would call out the names of people, who had given out their name, to ask for any comments, thoughts, or concerns and would then go around in the meeting room doing the same. When you address people by their names in a meeting or a crowd, people usually appreciate it. As Dale Carnegie wrote in his book 'How to win friends and influence people', a person's name is indeed the sweetest word in any language, for that person.

When you remember, and do not forget a person's name – even after you meet them after a long time, they will not forget you either. They will usually have kind thoughts towards you.

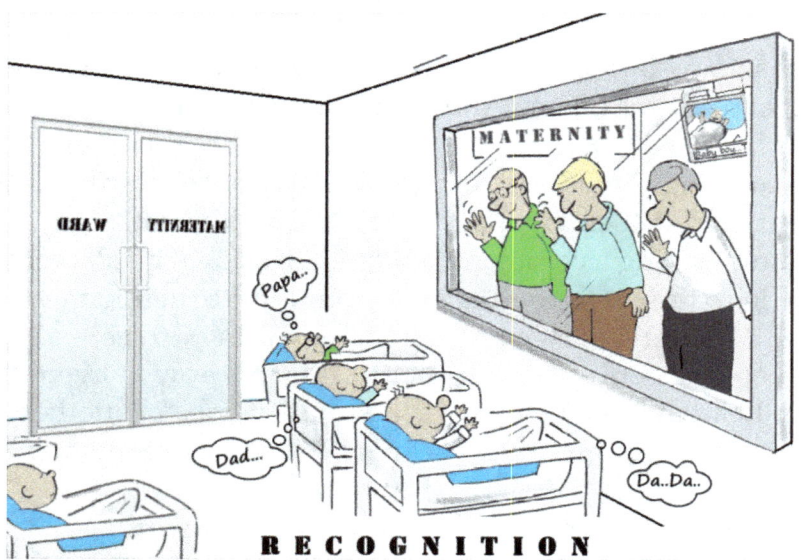

**R E C O G N I T I O N**

I felt that since I took the trouble to address people by their names, I did get extra consideration from them. And if I forgot someone's name I did not feel shy to ask them again, prefacing my question with the fact that I am working on my name-memory and asking them to repeat it.

I feel that this overall approach has helped me in life and as a manager.

# Find the Good in people and cultivate that

**TACT IS THE ABILITY TO DESCRIBE OTHERS AS THEY SEE THEMSELVES**
*~ Abraham Lincoln*

**PEOPLE DO NOT HAVE TO BE GOOD ALL THE WAY FOR YOU TO TREAT THEM WELL. REMEMBER WHAT YOU PUT OUT IS WHAT YOU GET BACK. THEY JUST NEED ONE GOOD THING IN THEM**
*~ Vikram Khushalani*

**THREE MONKEYS ONLY SEE GOOD IN PEOPLE**

Each one of us has good and bad qualities. Find the Good qualities in people and address and cultivate them. Make them the cornerstone of your relationship with them. This is important in both - the professional and the personal environments.

People like the recognition of good qualities in themselves by others. And when you recognize those qualities and associate those qualities with their being, they rise to the occasion and live up to those qualities.

I have chosen on my own, and often been handed staff, which was considered sub or low quality – as judged by others. I have always found some good in them and cultivated that good and I have had success and in the end, with sparkling jewels (so to speak) working with me. It has been an honor to work with them.

It also raises their self-esteem and self-confidence. It has worked wonders for the team morale and productivity. After all, I was considered below-par by some people when I was still green behind my ears, though I knew better. Once I found my footing, my confidence and capabilities increased.

I had an Art Teacher in junior school. Since Art was a mandatory subject (all subjects taught to us were mandatory) I wanted to shine in it. However my art skills were poor. So I went to my Art Teacher and appealed to him to make me a better art student, and ultimately an artist.

This was the first time that a student had approached him with such a request. And he was happy. So, the next time we had an art exercise in class, the sketching of tree right outside our class room, he walked over to me and asked me if I was willing to put in some extra effort. I nodded my concurrence.

He told me to complete my "tree sketching" and then to let him know. I finished my exercise and went up to him and showed him my work. He walked over to my easel, with me in tow, and faced the tree. He told me to half close my eyes and look towards the tree first and take in the whole scene. He asked me to see the surrounding beauty and appreciate it for a moment. Then he told me to turn my focus to the subject – the tree and study it 'dreamily' and only then start drawing. He put a fresh sheet of paper on my easel and asked me to begin the process.

As I took in the scenery and later studied the tree I found a depth and beauty in it that I had not observed before. Needless to say, it definitely improved my art exercise. It also made me realize that there is more to any object/subject than meets the initial glance. This incident made me realize the beauty and depth surrounding any, and every, entity.

My art did gradually improve, but it also gave me a new-found appreciation of beauty in the world around me. I also started applying this to my interaction with people around me. Some of my teachers (for whom I have tremendous respect) found the potential, and capabilities in me to help me further my education and life. I have applied the same principles to my dealings with other people to their, and mostly my, benefit.

# Strive to Excel in some Field

**EXCELLENCE IS THE GRADUAL RESULT
OF ALWAYS STRIVING TO DO BETTER**
*~ Pat Riley (NBA Coach)*

## SCHOOL WRESTLING RING

Right from my school days I was interested in martial arts. I learned at every opportunity I got. Back in those days we did not have martial arts schools like we do today. So I bought books on Jiu Jitsu, Judo, Karate, etc. I would read and visualize the various moves and practice with my friends.

Later on, while still in school, the moves I learned, turned
into street fighting techniques.  They became my self-defense
routines which I kept honing to the best of my abilities.   I
would not go and pick a fight with somebody, but they
became my defense in case someone picked on me.  These
techniques also became my reputation makers, so to speak.

I did get a chance to learn Indian Style Wrestling from a true,
and renowned, wrestler in the senior school years.  We had a
Physics Teacher, whom, we did not know and realize earlier,
was an accomplished wrestler.  He was built like a wrestler –
muscular, thick neck, flattened ears, but he was a very quiet
and unassuming person.  He was gentle and never
disciplined any student.  We therefore all used to enjoy his
class.  Students would throw balled up papers, chalk pieces,
rubber bands, etc. at each other, when his attention was
turned to the blackboard.  He knew but did not object due to
his leniency and calm nature as long as we did our
assignments and were quiet during his lecture.

One day he decided to start teaching wrestling, open only to
the senior grade students.  A lot of us signed up.  The first
day was a talk on 'code of conduct' and 'ethics', followed by
a demonstration with his senior pupil (who was a salaried
employee of the school, and a lab assistant in the school
chemistry lab).  The demonstration was awe inspiring for us.
He was smooth and fast like greased lightning. The next
day, during his class, there was pin-drop silence and we had
a new-found respect for him.  Gone were the paper throwing
and boisterous days.  We were all well behaved.

I became an ardent student of wrestling.  He offered me an
apprenticeship at his Akhaadaa (Dojo) that summer.  My
father did not permit me to join.  So he offered it to another
student, who had wanted to be professional wrestler.  That
student did join and later became a professional wrestler.

The one year that I learned wrestling from him, he inculcated some enduring habits in me. He taught by live example. He practiced his art every day. He controlled his emotions (anger, frustration, etc.) in the ring. He was always planning a few moves ahead. He taught us practice, practice till you can do it blindfolded. That was the key. All actions in the ring should become involuntary.

The key take away was, that the physics teacher excelled at something other than the subject he taught. He was not a gold medalist in Physics, or famous for his erudition in his subject. He excelled in something else.

Often you find that people are respected for their skill and excellence in something, even if it is not their main bread and butter. So, one should strive to excel in something, even if it is a hobby.

I knew a colleague who was interested in Ornithopters (according to the dictionary - a machine designed to achieve flight by means of flapping wings). And ornithopters come in various designs – some are designed to look like specific birds. I had read that an airport uses an ornithopter, designed to look like a predatory bird – they use this ornithopter to scare other birds away. They fly the ornithopter every time the birds are seen flying in larger numbers. This scares the birds away and increases the safety of plane.

I learnt about my colleague's interest in ornithopters when I got interested in them and heard from someone else about his interest. He was kind enough to bring a couple of them to the office and we went out to the parking lot during our lunch break and he demonstrated the various ornithopters.

Soon other people also expressed interest in his hobby and later on two people from the upper management also expressed interest.  Resulting in his getting exposure to, and being noticed by these upper management employees.  He ultimately moved to the department of one of the corporate managers with prospects of promotions.

It is like the golf club in a company.  Where people from all levels of employment like to play and be noticed or become friends with the upper management.

One is sure to increase one's respect, in the eyes of others, as one becomes knowledgeable, or one acquires a skill, or one becomes an expert, or one excels in something.  Besides getting respect from others, one will find a new value and an interest and meaning in life.

One is also sure to bolster one's self-esteem and self-respect. One is also likely going to expand one's social circle.

# Know your projects blindfolded

BLINDFOLDED, YOUR FEELINGS ARE ENHANCED. YOU SEE LESS, YOU SEE NOTHING, BUT YOU FEEL MORE. YOU FEEL EVERYTHING.

*~ Chloe Thurlow*

My interest in Martial Arts has continued through my life. It has also been my go-to exercise. I feel that it has allowed me to maintain a healthy lifestyle.

After graduating from school, as I entered into college, I learned a specific form of Martial Arts from a master. He was truly a master of his craft. He taught Kalaripayattu (one of India's, and they say world's, oldest martial arts). I concentrated on the Keetukaari of Koltharipayattu (the art of bamboo-staff-fighting and wooden implements, including goat/deer horn/antler devices called Maduvu).

The Maduvu was part of the fighting technique. It could be used in self-defense or as a weapon. In self-defense, one held one Maduvu in each hand and deflected the bamboo-staff attacks to the side of the body. As a weapon one used the pointed horns/antlers as a means of attack.

**Maduvu (usually a pair)**

I was fortunate to learn from him. I do not remember how I came to know of him and get in touch with him. He was blind, and he used to walk from a nearby village to my college to teach me. He could not see, he was totally blind, and had a young man, on whose shoulder he kept his hand and was led around. We made a rough ring, whose boundaries he mentally mapped with the young man walking around the boundary.

Once in the ring, no one could touch him. He did not need any visual aid/assistance. No matter whether you attacked with a stick or even threw/hurled a stick or something at him, he was deftly able to deflect in and defend himself and subdue an opponent. I had never seen anyone like him.

He would come in the evening and teach me well after sunset, until I stopped him, since I could not see in the darkening light. He used to teach me in an open field, behind my hostel. There were no lights.

While he taught me the art of bamboo-staff-fighting and self-defense, I marveled at his uncanny ability to sense without eye-sight.

I realized from observing and learning from him that one should be able to practice one's art literally 'Blindfolded'.

Ideally one should become so familiar with one's work, one's tasks, one's project, that one should be able to execute them without referring to any notes. One should know the road-map, the stakeholders, and track new issues utilizing known techniques. At least, that is how one should approach his/her job.

Try to never get caught off-guard when your senior corporate officers, or your clients, or any of your stakeholder, asks you a question about your projects. Know the ins and outs of your projects. One should know the Schedule, Resources allocations, expenditures, Budgeted Cost for Work Performed, the Budgeted Cost for Work Scheduled, the Earned Value, etc. Know the details and overall Project Status.

Often I would meet a visiting end client, or an upper-management corporate team member, and besides making small talk, would be asked specific questions about some project, or some issue, or an area of a project, task, or a contractor. It would not be proper to tell them that I would get back to them due to my inability to recall the status. So, be prepared, be ready.

One cannot know everything, but what is to be known, one should know by heart, and should be able to visualize blindfolded.

# Get Credentialed

CREDENTIALS ARE CRITICAL. IF YOU WANT TO DO
SOMETHING PROFESSIONAL. IF YOU WANT TO BECOME A
DOCTOR OR LAWYER OR TEACHER OR PROFESSOR,
THERE IS A CREDENTIALING PROCESS. BUT THERE ARE
A LOT OF OTHER THINGS WHERE IT'S NOT CLEAR
THEY'RE THAT IMPORTANT.
~ Peter Thiel

The interviewer asked 'Why should we hire you? What skills and assets will you bring to the company?' She was giving me an opportunity to tell them what set me apart from others. And it was my chance to tell them what distinguishes me.

I was applying for a Project Lead position. I had experience in leading teams (and I presume so did others applying for this same position). I mentioned my experience and the successes I had in my projects. I also mentioned my people skills, etc. She nodded but seemed to be wanting to hear more. They were obviously interested in hiring me but, as I learned later, they wanted a justification on why they should give me preference over others, where all the candidates seemed equal(ish).

I then highlighted the fact that I was a member of the Project Management Institute (PMI). And would soon be working on getting my Project Management Professional (PMP) certification. This was the magic word for her - Professional Credentials.

The PMP certification was just beginning to become popular. And while talking to this hiring manager, I realized that in a level playing field, certifications and credentials do give one an edge. I decided right there and then that I would actively work on getting my PMP certification. It turned out that it was actually going to be 11-12 years before I would move in that direction. Though that was not the intent at the time of the interview.

So, years after the interview - when I seriously contemplated getting my PMP certification, it seemed a very daunting task. I searched the Internet for tips and recommendations from others who had passed and shared their experience. I also considered taking one of the courses promising a 'guaranteed pass'. These courses were not cheap.

I knew a couple of people who had gone various routes and there did not seem to be any one sure shot method. I finally decided to study on my own and then tried to narrow my approach. So, I am presenting here the way I went about it. By God's grace I was able to pass and get my PMP certification on my first attempt.

I was already a member of the Project Management Institute (PMI). They are the ones who provide that certification. And there is an advantage of being a member of PMI when you are appearing for the exam since the exam fees are lower for members.

As a member benefit, I got the 'Project Management Body of Knowledge' (PMBOK) guide for free. The PMBOK guide provides the framework for the Project Management Practice. It is not a how-to but what-to guide. It is an amazing essential source for studying for the PMP certification.

Personally, I find the PMBOK guide to be very dry reading, I will admit that I never read it like a text book, but rather used it as a reference. After some research I decided on the 'Pass the PMP exam on your first try', from Velociteach.

I am sharing what worked for me. It took me two months to prepare for, and pass the exam. During the first month I basically studied for 1-2 hours, in the evenings, 2-3 days a week. I read the Velociteach book during that time, from cover to cover.

The author has done a fantastic job of interpreting the PMBOK guide and making it an easier read. He also provides quizzes at the end of each chapter and a test exam at the end of the book.

The author includes an online resource for additional tests. Which, by the way, I did not use since, after all my studies, I felt prepared and ready.

The PMBOK guide provides a table of 'Knowledge Areas' intersecting with 'Functional Areas'. It is necessary to understand them and memorize them at a higher level. I printed a copy of that page and used it as a ready reference. And during the time I was preparing for my exam, I would mentally go over the Knowledge/Functional area table, as I lay down to sleep. Often I fell asleep during that process, but it became ingrained in my mind. I would relate to the Knowledge/Functional areas from my professional experience, tying them to various phases of my current and past projects.

As I progressed through my preparation and read the Earned Value Management (EVM) section, I could relate that to my job experience since we used that on a day-to-day basis. I also practiced the various problems presented in the book. I would also sometimes look for an EVM problem on the Internet and try to solve it.

After going through the book once, I took the practice exam presented at the end of the book. It was not a great score. So I scanned the book, trying to refresh/strengthen my weak areas. A few day later I again took the same practice exam with very encouraging, and improved, results.

I spent a few more days surfing the Internet looking for, and attempting to answer PMP exam questions. I think that a lot of people are gracious to post PMP questions and answers, in order to help others.

I finally took my PMP exam. It turned out to be based more on practical knowledge than theoretical. The mathematical problems, and knowing the formulae, were helpful in adding to the overall score. The problems were not complex, but it is strongly recommended that one works out as many practice problems as one has time to. One can find practice problems on the Internet.

# When you maintain your Credentials you will maintain your edge

**HEROES NEED MONSTERS TO ESTABLISH THEIR HEROIC CREDENTIALS. YOU NEED SOMETHING SCARY TO OVERCOME.**
*~ Margaret Atwood*

Every job type has some credentials or certification or training in order to enhance one's skill set and knowledge. The best teacher is of course experience.

A lot of certifications and/or professions have credentials that need to be renewed, maintained, or updated periodically. The medical profession is an example, where knowledge and techniques get dated (outdated) and need to be renewed. The same is true for the Project Management discipline. So, this applies to 'PMP', the 'PRINCE2 Practitioner', and the Certified Project Director (CPD) ™, amongst others.

This chapter is of special interest for those who are certified and/or credentialed in their field. For others, it is hoped that they will be encouraged and strongly consider getting certified in their field of practice, or interest.

When my PMP certification needed to be renewed, I turned to the internet to research different ways to earn Professional Development Units (PDUs) so I could maintain my PMP credentials for another three years. For PMP certification renewal one needs to earn 60 PDUs during the period that one's PMP certification is valid. One has to be careful to earn these PDUs before one's certification elapses.

PMI offers two type of PDUs one can earn in order to renew one's certification - *Education* and *Giving Back to the Profession*. I chose to earn my PDUs largely in the Education arena.

Earning *Giving Back to the Profession* can be accomplished in one of the following ways:
- Work as a Practitioner
- Create Content
- Give a Presentation
- Share Knowledge
- Volunteer

Earning *Education* PDUs can be accomplished in the following ways:

- Course or Training
- Organization Meetings
- Online or Digital Media
- Reading
- Informal Learning

A lot of people have shared the different ways to earn PDUs and I want to mention that for 'Education' PDUs there are two main sites I used which offer free Webinars - Corporate Education Group (www.corpedgroup.com) and the Project Management com (ProjectManagement.com) website.

I again had to renew my PMP Credentials in 2021, since one has to renew every 3 years. This time I used the following two sites: (1) "The Project Management Podcast". Their website is www.project-management-podcast.com; (2) "Institute for Leadership Excellence & Development Inc." Their website is www.peopleandprojectspodcast.com

As you earn PDUs you have to go to PMI's online Continuing Certification Renewal System (CCRS) to report PDUs and also to view your certification records when you want to. This allows you, and PMI, to keep a record of your PDU's and inform you once you have met the requirements for renewal.

It is a good idea to listen to the Webinars, Podcasts, etc. from time-to-time, even if one does not need to renew one's PMI Credentials. It broadens one's perspective and views. It is also good to listen to other people's experiences and views. One enriches one's knowledge.

Re-certification also adds knowledge, techniques, evolving management processes, new technology, and new thought processes which have been added to field since your last certification. There may also be certain things one has forgotten, because of disuse.

# Be Compassionate

**BE KIND, FOR EVERYONE YOU MEET IS FIGHTING A HARDER BATTLE.**
*~ Plato*

A manager faces many situations when he/she needs to make a decision which will have a short term, or a long term, impact on the staff, colleagues, senior management, clients, or competitors. A lot of decision even affect one's Vendors and Suppliers. Always be just, maintain your integrity, but above all - be Compassionate.

Let me give a staff example - JJ was a Senior Engineer, on my team, who had worked for the company for over 30 years, since the company's early development days. Now the company had over 60,000 employees. He was close to retirement. He was also dealing with a handicap. The senior manager decided that we should let him go (since he probably thought we could hire a junior person, with a lower salary). So, he approached me and suggested that.

While the senior manager was kind of right in his thinking, and he was not responsible for either the budget or the tasking, since it was my team, I was the one responsible for these things. However, he was not, by any means, acting compassionately. I did not tell him what I was thinking, but told him that I would get back to him.

I had a discussion with the JJ, the Senior Engineer, and suggested to him to take on some additional tasking by doing some price-performance analysis for all the tasks we had in our team, based on corporate project history, and some recommendations (drawing on his experience) to improve the bottom line, without impacting quality. This was the kind of information that the senior management would value and a junior engineer may not be able to provide. I also asked JJ to monitor defects and ensure that they did not exceed established thresholds by our Quality Assurance procedures.

I then proceeded to inform the senior manager who had proposed laying-off the engineer. He was happy with the way the things had turned out. Later he was even happier to receive the reports.

Problem solved. JJ announced a year later, on his own, that he was retiring, and left under his own steam and his own time frame.

Another example - CD was a Software Developer and also a Software Architect. She was also a heavy smoker. She came and told me once that she wanted to quit her job. I asked her if whether she would be willing to share the reason. She told me after some deliberation that she had a health issue related to her lungs.

She could not function any more. She had to have surgery right away. And it was debatable whether the surgery would successfully resolve the issue.

I suggested that she apply for a long-term leave based on her health. I would take the request to the management and try to get it approved. And if God-willing she recovered well enough, to come back, she would have a job waiting for her. And if she did not want to come back, or was unable to do so, she could then tender her resignation in at that time. In the mean time I would hold off on hiring a replacement for her, if I could help it until that time when I absolutely needed to. In which case I would check with her on her health before proceeding. I also suggested that she keep the office appraised (or me appraised - if that was her comfort level) periodically, and on a regular basis.

It turned out that she was able to recover well from her surgery and returned to work 3 months later.

She got her job back and the team benefitted by her experience and knowledge. I also noticed that she was far more enthusiastic after her return.

# Protect Your Team

**GREAT MINDS DISCUSS IDEAS; AVERAGE MINDS DISCUSS EVENTS;**
**SMALL MINDS DISCUSS PEOPLE**
*~ Elanor Roosevelt*

Insulate your team from office politics. Office politics has a negative effect on the team. What should the team concentrate on – their work, or other trifle issues (like office politics) which sap their energy?  So, protect and insulate your team from office politics. Let them concentrate on the tasks they have been assigned, or undertaken. Let them fulfill their assigned duties without having to worry about office-politics. That is your worry, the manager's worry (if at all). It is your duty to protect your team from this time-wasting, non-productive, and unfruitful activity.

Protect your team from even their colleagues, if you are able
to.  Refer to the chapter on '**Learn the Business**', where I
provided an example of how I protected my staff from
getting on to bad terms with their Labor Union.

Expose and encourage them instead, to first concentrate on
their jobs and assignment completion, and on developing
their skills. Or sharpening the ones they already have.  Get
them the option of in-house training (where available) or
client sponsored training (where the client has been willing
to provide it), or even vendor provided training courses
(Refer to the chapter on '**Staff Readiness**', on some tips on
getting Vendors to provide training for their products).

Where there are people there will be politics.  This is a way
of life. And once your staff realizes that you go out of the
way to protect them and insulate them from office politics,
they will be ready to go to bat for you and the project.

While you are doing your duty as a manager, they will feel a
certain loyalty towards you and the project.

# Do Not Hold Grudges

FORGIVE OTHERS, NOT BECAUSE THEY DESERVE
FORGIVENESS, BUT BECAUSE YOU DESERVE PEACE.
~ *Jonathan Lockwood Huie*

I had woe against my foe
I told it not and it began to grow
I had woe against my friend
I told it and so it went

In the office environment one comes across situations which
can lead to mental conflicts. The first thing to remember is
not to make it personal. And try not to harbor any grudges.
Grudges do make it personal and one loses the right
perspective.

I had learned a long time ago that if there is such a situation,
which seems to be conflagratory in nature, it is often best to
confront it face to face, and discuss it openly with the person
who has been the cause of it.

Sometimes expressing it openly clears misunderstanding (if there is any). Or lets the other person know how you feel.

Once you express your feelings they are not bottled up inside you and it will make you feel better. This is more so, when you are dealing with people who are friendly towards you and even if they are not, sometimes it converts them to have a friendly outlook towards you.

Holding grudges can be bad for your health and peace of mind. It is like Road Rage – it makes a person angry when someone cuts one off on the road, or makes an obscene gesture at someone. One may get angry and start chasing the other person, but pause for a moment and think – you are probably never going to see this person again. Let it go.

I remember once I was driving on a local highway, going to work, when a car cut me off. The person cut in front of me, very close – I though the car might hit me. I got very angry and sped up and started chasing the person. My heart was beating very fast because of my anger and adrenalin.

As I continued to chase the car, I suddenly I felt as if some 'bitter liquid drops' were squeezed from an area, above my heart, and were oozing into my heart. I did not know what it was, but I realized that if I continued to get enraged, it would be injurious to my health, and probably my heart. I slowed down to my normal driving speed and discontinued my pursuit of the car. I often remember that incident when I am faced with a similar situation.

# HOLDING A GRUDGE

## IS LIKE HOLDING A POISON
## IN YOUR HEART

It does not pay to hold grudges, even for a short time. They say 'Let go and let God'.

# Be a hard act to follow

**I'M A HARD ACT TO FOLLOW, BECAUSE WHEN I'M DONE, I TAKE THE MICROPHONE WITH ME.**
*~ Mitch Hedberg*

In life, one should try to be the best at what one does. Not just in terms of the quality of your work, but also in getting the job done, staying the course, ensuring that all stakeholders are engaged and involved. Do things with a smile, and genuinely feel happy that you are given an opportunity to do this work and consider it a privilege granted to you.

Since our project team was always pro-active and made every effort to finish tasks ahead of time, if not just on time, the client was very impressed with our team. The client would often approach our corporate management and drop a hint that they would prefer some team like ours, to get involved and execute an upcoming task.

This was due to fact that our project team provided them value, in return, for every dollar of the budget, the client allocated to our project.

We habitually, told the client when we have saved on the cost, that we had some leftover budget, that they, the client, could utilize that saving in such-and-such task, or in training, etc. This was an investment for them, and the client would often add more funding to the suggested, or upcoming task and send it our way. It was a win-win situation for all involved.

Remember that your stakeholders include the staff that works on it. So, try to be available and willing to help them complete their tasks. Let them remember your compassion and understanding in their interaction with you, the tasks, and the workplace.

Every task, every action of yours should get 110% of your attention and effort. When one devotes one's full attention to a task, then one does not have to go back and make adjustments. Some task do require fine-tuning, but in general if you do your tasks well then you do not have to correct them.

Try to make every task you perform as a task well done. Make near perfection, a hallmark, a signature of the way you perform task.

I say 'near perfection' because truly speaking, we all cannot do things to perfection, though we can certainly strive for perfection. Let us make a resolve and an effort to do things well.

Let people remember you for being a problem solver, a person with answers. Let them remember your integrity and pleasant demeanor. Try to be the person who is missed when he/she is not there. Let us strive to be an act which is 'Hard To Follow and emulate'. So that we are always spoken highly of and our stakeholders always look forward to working with us. Always be your individual, sincere and exemplary self.

**BE YOURSELF, IT'S A TOUGH ACT TO FOLLOW.**
*~ Katharine Hepburn*

# Build an all-rounder Team

**I'M SURROUNDED BY NOTHING BUT GREAT PEOPLE. I'VE BEEN BLESSED WITH THAT, SO REALLY, I'VE GOT NO CHOICE BUT TO BE AN ALL-AROUND GOOD PERSON.**
*~ Tim Duncan*

Train your team so each team member acquires many skills relevant to typical projects you handle. Give them opportunities so they gain working knowledge, and better still, in some cases, expertise in job-related skills.

People usually love to expand their horizon and enhance their job-marketability. I used to provide such opportunities to staff and that was another attraction corporate staff had in working on my team.

This benefitted both, the staff and the project. With each staff member having more than one skill, the project was never out-of-luck when a staff member, say with Configuration Management skill, was out of the office. Or if the Technical Writers were not available. This way our team's delivery of software products was never held back when the formal testers were not available to test our products, since our team members were not only equipped to conduct testing, but had the skills to properly document testing of the products.

For the staff members, it made them more valuable on our team, or they could transfer to another team if they so desired. They realized that it also helped them in the job market since they had other skills, or even if they were interested in moving up the career ladder or to switch to management positions.

I also involved my team members in product evaluations, product performance, and product marketing, to name a few. I however made sure that in my effort to make my team members all-rounders, I was always ensuring that their work, deadlines, etc. never suffered.

Many times my staff members would come and confide in me that they would like to move towards a specific field, and ultimately transition full time, into it. I made it a point to help them acquire the skills related to their chosen field, as far as I could help them.

I have worn almost all hats in my Management, Engineering, and Information Technology career. It was not because people wanted to help me, but it was because they had a need in those areas and my skills met their criteria at that time.

I wanted to be different and I wanted to help my team reach their goals, as they were helping me reach mine, in the corporate and specific portfolio arena.

# Do Not Become Indispensable

**DON'T THINK OF YOURSELF AS INDISPENSABLE OR INFALLIBLE. AS CHARLES DE GAULLE SAID, THE CEMETERIES OF THE WORLD ARE FULL OF INDISPENSABLE MEN.**
*~ Donald Rumsfeld*

**Contrary** to popular advice – don't make yourself "Indispensable". Make yourself "Dependable", the person who gets the job done no matter how difficult or complex it is. Make yourself 'Missed' when you are not there.

When a person is "Indispensable" one cannot get away from the office. One cannot take vacations. And people around you will become complacent. They will not be motivated to do the work themselves.

And let us not kid ourselves – we all know that no one is "Indispensable". When we think that we are indispensable, we are only fooling ourselves and we are taking ourselves too seriously. Projects and life will go on even if we are not there. This also means that you have to let those employees know, who think that they are indispensable due to some skill or knowledge they have, that it is not the case.

So, I made it a point to subtly let the people around me know, in various ways. That included the management chain above me. I let people know that they were valuable, but no one was indispensable – including me.

Many times, someone who is considered to be indispensable, is passed up when it comes to promotion time. As an example, one of the companies I worked for, had a senior developer who had authored a payroll program, written in Common Business Oriented Language (COBOL). He was very intelligent and smart, but the management was reluctant to promote him or move him to a lead position of another group, because he was managing that payroll program so well and since he understood the intrinsic details, they did not want to move him out.

He confided in me one day about his concern that he was not getting promoted due to his expertise in that one 'critically important' payroll program. On top of that the COBOL computer language was slowly losing usage since it was very verbose and, he thought, clunky. He could leave the company, for another job, but did not want to do it since the company had been good to him and catered to his personal needs (leave, vacations, etc.), and his commute to work was very short.

I suggested that he go to management and suggest that they authorize funds for the re-write of the program in a modern language, like the 'C' Programming Language in order to modernize it and also to make it more maintainable, since 'C' programming language programmers were more readily available than the COBOL language, which seemed to be on its way out as a computer language. (Just a note – even to this day there are a few legacy programs which have been written in the COBOL language and are being maintained by the companies which use them). I also suggested that he write some common maintenance procedures for the converted program so that the critically important program gets appropriate documentation. I further suggested that he design the new program to be modular in structure so that maintenance can be easier.

I added that he would also gain new skills as he re-writes the program in a more modern language. So, he did go and talk to management. They told him that they would think about it.

Independently, to help him and also myself, I went and talked to the client (US Army), specifically my counterpart, about modernizing their software, which this company was maintaining for them. I suggested that they, my counterpart, take this up to his upper management, to invest in the modernization, and modularization, of the software.

In the end it all worked out for everyone. The client agreed to fund the modernization of not just that program but some others on the critical list. Our company authorized the funds internally to re-work that program and others like it. I was thanked by the client, by our corporate management, and my colleague and I, each got individual promotions in the process.

On your projects, make sure that you do not become 'Indispensable' either. Train a few selected staff members to take over your responsibilities, when you are out of the office. Your deputy project manager should not only be the second in the chain of command, but she/he should be able to carry out the project tasks in your absence. The deputy project manager should also have the authority to act on your behalf and take decisions, for the good, and for the timely, execution of the project.

In case you are concerned that you might became easily replaceable when you train a single person in your responsibilities, then have a team of (at least) three, senior staff members, who can collectively take care of project business.

Remember that you are not replaceable though. You have unique characteristics and traits that cannot be replicated. Provided, of course, you have acted like yourself and not mimicked someone else, to get where you are. You are a unique individual, so develop yourself as such and behave in that manner accordingly.

# Delegate - Delegate – Delegate

THE FIRST RULE OF MANAGEMENT IS DELEGATION. DON'T TRY
AND DO EVERYTHING YOURSELF BECAUSE YOU CAN'T.
*~ ANTHEA TURNER, BRITISH MEDIA PERSONALITY*

WHEN YOU DELEGATE TASKS, YOU CREATE
FOLLOWERS. WHEN YOU DELEGATE AUTHORITY,
YOU CREATE LEADERS.
*~ CRAIG GROESCHEL, FOUNDER OF LIFE CHURCH*

THE BEST EXECUTIVE IS THE ONE WHO HAS SENSE ENOUGH
TO PICK GOOD MEN TO DO WHAT HE WANTS DONE, AND
SELF-RESTRAINT TO KEEP FROM MEDDLING WHILE THEY
DO IT.
*~ THEODORE ROOSEVELT, 26TH U.S. PRESIDENT*

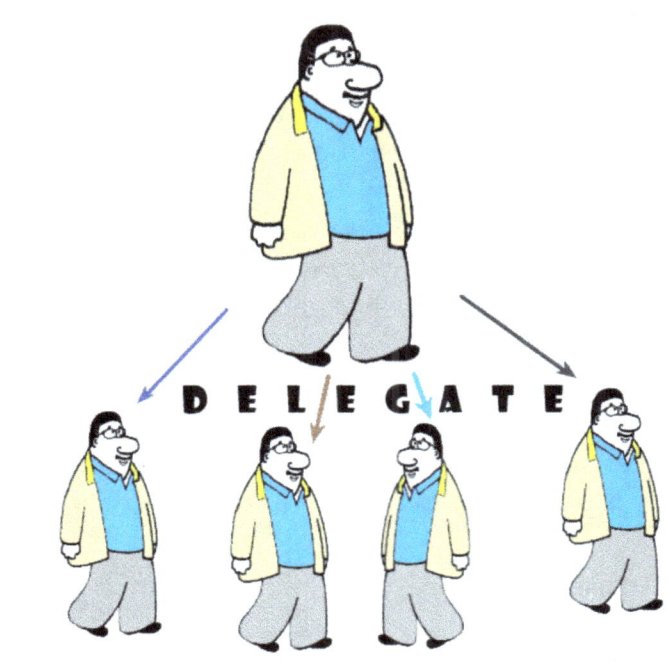

Gary had a refreshing approach to management. He oversaw the project I managed. He left it on me as to how I managed the project. He never, never, micromanaged. He never crowded anyone who worked on his programs. He delegated the day-to-day management of projects in his portfolio, to assigned managers.

He would let a person know what was expected and then let them do their thing. One could always go to him for clarification or verification, if one wanted to. He monitored the results without interfering. He knew how to delegate.

As a manager you have to learn to trust your staff enough to delegate a task, project, or a program. In order to achieve that state of confidence in your team, you have to give them opportunities to improve their capabilities. Help them if they flounder, guide them when needed. Once you have delegated a task to them, do not interfere in their operation.

Wendell was just the opposite of Gary. He was a technical person made a manager and we were a team consisting of Software Engineers, Software Developers, Testers, etc. I was a software consultant at that time, developing code in the 'C' programming language. A programming language I was not very experienced in. My client knew that and even though I was reluctant to accept the position, the client requested me to accept it with the assurance that they would overlook my lack of experience and allow me to grow into it.

As it turned out, the team had greater problems and issues to deal with. The project became Wendell's life. He would spend 12-18 hours in the office. He would demand an end of the day report from each person, before the person went home.

He would then surreptitiously make changes to the software code written by the individual team members to the way he thought it ought to work, or how he thought it should be coded. He would usually not tell the person that he had made changes, and would admit to it only after he was confronted.

The code modules did not function as they were designed to work and had been coded, all due to the changes Wendell had made. This was due to the fact that Wendell did not have time to read comments, design notes and changes that were made to interfaces. As result the project was headed to a disastrous end.

The staff complained to upper management. After due deliberation, the upper management, very wisely I might add, removed Wendell from the position and the project struggled to meet its deadlines, and after missing a few, was able to recover in the end.

Wendell was micromanaging. He did not trust the team and even after the 'de-facto delegation' to the developers to develop code by the team members, he tried to interfere and do stuff himself with near disastrous results for the project. It also affected the morale and trust of the team members.

The 'Gary delegation model' compared to the 'Wendell delegation model' are a stark contrast on how 'to-do' and how 'not-to-do' delegation.

When we delegate a task or a job to someone, we give them an opportunity to grow and develop leadership skills. We cultivate, in them, management and leadership skills. This is the most important aspect. It gives them some achievements to be proud of and learn from.

The secondary benefit is that it allows us to turn our attention to other activities and progress other issues. The more we become adept in 'delegation' the more our horizon opens up to achieve more in a day.

In order to delegate some responsibilities to others we have to train them to handle those things we are delegating to them. We have to impart the basic knowledge to them.

On my projects, there was always a backup for me. Besides the Deputy PM, there were engineers, analysts, architects, who were aware of the various aspects of the projects. And they did rise to the occasion, when the opportunity arose.

Delegation is a crucial management skill.

# Cross-Train your Team Members

**TRAIN PEOPLE WELL ENOUGH SO THEY CAN LEAVE, TREAT THEM WELL ENOUGH SO THEY DON'T WANT TO.**
*~ Sir Richard Branson*

By cross-training your team members you effectively create a back-up person for each team member. This will make your team resilient, even when one team member is unable to work on an assigned task.

With a cross-trained team you can also add support to a task with a cross-trained employee on hand. Depending on the size of your team and the tasks, you can assign one, or more, backups for each task. The backup person has to become familiar, at a higher level, not a detailed day-to-day level since that person has her/his own tasks to perform on a daily basis.

This is different from a back-up person. With a back-up person one has a dedicated staff member backing up the primary person. In cross-training, one has more staff flexibility, since any cross-trained employee can lend a helping hand in case of a need.

This also assures the stakeholders that the work will continue despite personnel disruptions, even though the disruptions may be planned or unplanned. When they are planned – they could be a temporary or permanent staff re-assignment due to various causes. When they are unplanned, they could be temporary re-assignment, due to short term disruptions. In either case the stakeholders and senior management are assured continuity of operations.

> **THE ONLY THING WORSE THAN TRAINING EMPLOYEES AND LOSING THEM, IS TO NOT TRAIN THEM AND KEEP THEM.**
> *~ Zig Ziglar*

In order to cross-train your employees you have to plan for it before you can begin. First you have to get a buy-in from all your stakeholders (staff, upper management, vendors, and most importantly your customers). I sold this to my customers by telling them that their work will not be interrupted due staff latency. I also offered training a limited number of their staff. They readily approved the approach.

One will also have to consider the following:

Cross Training Plan (CTP)
Project Plan review
Budget

Scope
Schedule
Documentation
Staff assignments
Periodic Review

## Cross Training Plan

The Cross Training Plan (CTP) should chalk out the remaining items and how one will go about it. So, it should include the Project Plan review, Budget, Scope, Schedule, Documentation, Staff assignments, and Periodic Review).

The CTP need not be voluminous, but it should touch the key points and assess their impact and lay out the approach/particulars. It should also have a start schedule point and a schedule end point.

## Project Plan review

The entire Project Plan should be reviewed for Budget, Scope, Schedule, etc. at a project level and team level. Cross-Training should become an integral part of the Project Plan so it does not impact the project's budget and schedule negatively. The Project Plan should be reviewed for prioritization of teams requiring/benefitting the most from the cross-training. For example those projects on the Critical-Path should be given higher priority than others for their respective teams receiving cross-training.

The CTP, within the Project Plan, has to have stakeholder concurrence for its success. Cross training will have an impact on the scope and budget, but if it is planned for, then its impact is accounted for already.

**Budget**

The budget for Cross Training should be included in the CTP. Many customers appreciate this forethought in planning and action.

As you estimate and calculate the budget, contact your technology/product vendors and enquire whether they offer some no-cost training. Even if they do not – talk to a manager there to see if you can arrange free training. I have been able to sell free-training to vendors by pointing out that it is in their interest to provide some training. Your clients will be more open to approving the final budget if any free training is included, or you have at least tried to get a vendor to provide you one.

**Schedule**

Consider Cross Training as a mini project, with all the planning that goes into a project. Look at the overall schedule and plan this Cross Training to fit into the overall Project Schedule (Master Schedule).

**Documentation**

The original documentation would be a good starting point, and one can re-purpose relevant sections of the existing project documentation related to the technology portion and know-how.

The CTP documentation should also contain 'who, when, where, and how' of the Cross Training. One should also include how the sharing on the existing documentation, and on-going information-exchange regarding the current project tasks, and the Software Engineers will be accomplished. The schedule will address the 'when' question.

The Cross Training Documentation should have all relevant Defect Register, Defect Resolution, the Risk Register, and how the cross-trained staff will have access to it.

## Staff Assignments

The Staff Assignments should be made so there are cross-training opportunities for all staff members, including yourself (the Project Manager). This will also provide backup coverage in each area.

If you can afford the time, the staff should not be loaded "to the hilt" with their primary tasks only. They should be afforded the time (in the schedule) to cross train.

Often, staff will express an interest in working on a different sub-task rather than their primary one. This will make your task easier for the sake of cross training assignment. The staff member will also be happy to work, as a backup and to cross train in the sub-task of their choice.

## Periodic Review

Periodic Reviews are an essential part of Cross Training. They let you know how well the Cross Training is working.

A high level review can first be conducted to assess the success of the program. It will also be a gauge of how the primary tasks are being affected by the cross training.

Then a review should be conducted at an individual level with each staff member to assess how each person is dealing with, and handling the cross training assignments personally. It is truthful and sincere to remind the staff that the cross training, while ensuring the continuity of the project, the schedule, and goal, is also helping the staff enhance their skills and that it is building a team that works well together. They are helping the project, each other, and themselves.

# Project Management Office

**PROJECT MANAGERS ARE THE MOST
CREATIVE PROS IN THE WORLD;
WE HAVE TO FIGURE OUT EVERYTHING
THAT COULD GO WRONG, BEFORE IT DOES.**
*~ Fredrick Haren*

**I AM DOING JUST WHAT I AM NOT BEING TOLD**
*~ Loisje*

The Project Management Office (PMO) is a group or department that defines and maintains standards for project management within the organization. Every organization does not have a PMO. Often it is a loosely-knit group of senior managers, who maintain project management standards within the organization.

Ask for the formulation of one, if your company does not have one. In the meantime, be your PMO and establish certain project management standards, which you follow, should follow, and strive for. These standards should be maintained for each project you undertake.

A PMO, in an organization, should be your friend and guide. Sometimes, your working style and work ethic can help shape your PMO.

In his book "The Complete Project Management Office Handbook" (Second Edition) Gerard Hill of The Hill Consulting Group has outlined five PMO functional areas:

-Practice Management
-Infrastructure Management
-Resource integration Management
-Technical support
-Business Development

He also lists 20 sub-functional areas within these five. Ensuring that a PMO becomes a business solution.

There is also a very interesting article -

Setting a PMO for the first time? No PM experience? Wow them in 100 days!
March 20, 2017 - Written by Hussain Bandukwala

He talks about a PMO leader who did not have Project Management Experience but set a PMO in 100 days. He says that PMO Leader's job is to:

- Set standards and governance
- Align the project portfolio to the organization's strategies
- Prove the need and value of the PMO
- Support one's team by removing roadblocks out of their way

I have seen very few organizations with a PMO. Usually the PMO functions are carried out by Senior Management [Program Manager(s), VPs, etc.], who set the standards, maintain Project Artifacts, past proposal efforts, Project Audits, etc.

Often Senior Managers provide mentoring to select managers who, in their opinion, have the qualifications and capabilities, to become leaders. And if one is interested in rising up the management chain then that is one avenue one should explore. Once an approach a senior manager and express one's interest.

One should not hesitate to express one's desire, or any suggestions that one has for improving the company's project performance. In order to do that one has to observe which senior manager appears to be influential and more inclined to promote others. Be cautious though, that you do not give your immediate manager the feeling that you are trying to skip, or go over, their head in order to satisfy your agenda.

The PMO Office

I learned long time ago, when I was working as a consultant, that if you make your manager feel good about you, he/she will promote your ambitions. Always make them look good, by being professional and loyal to their (which should also be the company's) progress and for the corporate good.

# Become a Mentor

*TEACH - AND YOU WILL LEARN*
*~ Vikram Khushalani*

I switched my career from Electrical Engineering to the Information Technology (IT) field after having worked as an Electrical Engineer for five years. I attended the Control Data Institute to study Computer Programming and started my first job in the industry as an Associate Programmer.

Besides learning how computers work, I learnt to program in Assembler, Common Business Oriented Language (COBOL), Formula Translation (FORTRAN), Pascal, PS2, etc. computer programming languages.

And we would create Punch Cards, which then were fed into a computer which, in turn, read the deck of those 'Punched Cards'.

If there was a mistake, even if a period or comma was input incorrectly, or out of place, we had to correct and run the cards again through the Punch Card Reader. This was very cumbersome.

On my first day of the job, as a programmer/developer, I was handed a hefty stack of about 300 pages, of a program written in COBOL and asked me to add sections in it where a Title and Date would be printed on each printed page output. Looking at the program I was lost and could not make out where I could add my new lines of code.

I remember clearly, looking around and selecting a programmer, who seemed to have a kind face and seemed to be a senior employee and turning to him for help to get me started. He very kindly spent an hour, or so, explaining the flow of the code and suggesting two places where my new code could go. That is all the help I needed to get started. I needed to be shown how in the practical world the program code flowed.

I became a lead programmer in the company in short order and the company, literally, doubled my salary at my first annual review. I have not forgotten the help and guidance I received, from my first mentor in the IT field. He and I became good friends as time passed, but most of all, that example helped me formulate a mentoring attitude towards others, who needed help.

Later on, when someone else needed help and I started helping and sort-of teaching, the person asked questions – some I could answer, the others I could not and had to refer to books to answer. I realized then that by teaching, I had discovered some gaps in my knowledge, and I had to fill those gaps in my knowledge about the subject.

This made my understanding of the subject also deeper. As I taught, I also filled in the gaps and cracks in my understanding.

This is what mentoring does, it benefits both – the Mentor and the Mentee.

We have to understand that we did not get to where we are today by ourselves. Somebody helped us, someone supported us, and someone gave freely, or we had to pay for it. In either case, we needed help. We need help from the day we are born. So, by Mentoring and helping, we are paying society back. It is our duty.

When we give, we get; when we teach, we too deepen our understanding and in turn learn.

### YOU HAVEN'T LEARNED IT UNTIL YOU CAN TEACH IT.
### ~ Rigel J Dawson

I had a professional friend. We used to remain in touch via LinkedIn. One day he told me that he is going to retire. I wrote to him after a month and asked him when he was going to retire, he replied to me that he would retire the following month. So I asked him if he would be willing to share how he marketed himself since he was a Vice President (VP)? He wrote back he would share and gave me an 800 telephone number, asking me to call him in a week.

I was suspicious since it was an 800 number, but we had been colleagues in the past and still were (I thought) good friends. I called the number reluctantly, and it kept ringing, without any one answering. My suspicion was confirmed. I wrote to him about this, but he never responded.

The reason I am mentioning this is that, when someone asks for your guidance, give it freely, and do not hold back, unless you have a valid reason. The reason could be that the person asking is your competitor. The person could be after your job, or your product. The person could be in your company or a competing company.

Let me give you an example – when I was working as a consultant, the company had hired another person. This person was in the cubicle next to mine (yes – we were consultants). This person was a rookie, but eager to learn and I was willing to mentor him.

One day I asked him what were his professional goals? He told me bluntly that he was after my job. I took that as a joke and continued to mentor him.

## Mentor's Mentor

Well you know that peopled who work in cubicles, cannot keep secrets for long.

And so his secret came out and was told to me by the person, on the other side of his cubicle. He was doing consulting for another company, on this company's time and resources.

He would ask me a question not relating to our company's business but relating to a different application. I had first thought that he was taking a course, so he would ask questions. But the person on the other side of his cubicle told me that he had heard him talking to some other person and give advice to that person on what to do, etc.

I was in a fix, this person was not being ethical by consulting for someone else on this company's time and resources. I was pondering over what I should do, but providence took over. Other people came to know what he was doing and someone complained to his supervisor. The supervisor in turn, went to a cubicle nearby and overheard him talking to the other company. He was confronted by his supervisor and shortly thereafter, let go.

Had I known before that he was not being ethical and that he was learning from me to consult with another company, utilizing this company's resources, I would not have helped him. One learns as one goes along in his/her life.

# Plan for 'Continuity of Operations' and 'Disaster Recovery'

**WE CANNOT STOP NATURAL DISASTERS BUT WE CAN ARM OURSELVES WITH KNOWLEDGE: SO MANY LIVES WOULDN'T HAVE TO BE LOST IF THERE WAS ENOUGH DISASTER PREPAREDNESS.**
*~ Petra Nemcova*

Even if your project is not critical, always plan for 'Continuity of Operations' in case of a Disaster. And also chalk out how you will perform Disaster Recovery. Disaster does not strike after it announces its intent, so be prepared.

In order to do that you have to plan your activities in case of a catastrophic disaster. Whether it is due to natural causes, or it is due to willful attack on the integrity and operations of your system. And you have to determine system thresholds of tolerable impacts and design your systems to exceed those thresholds

There is great wisdom in what Gen. H. Norman Schwarzkopf once said "The more you sweat in peace, the less you bleed in war". So, the more you practice 'Disaster Recovery' the less you will suffer in case such an eventuality occurs.

Part of the planning would include taking backups of your system and data at regular intervals and just prior to testing and deploying major Project Releases. This said – one should develop a plan for Disaster Recovery and for Continuing Operations, even as you are conducting recovery from your disaster.

I have seen that once you let the stakeholders know that this is what you are planning, they will ensure the availability of resources for such operations. The resources may include equipment, skills, and possibly people.

If your company has such a processes in place, then one should endeavor to become a part of the process, be included in it. It would be beneficial to study the company's Disaster Recovery plan (if they have one) or develop your own. Once the plan is developed then conduct a test and a dry-run of the plan to see its viability and team preparedness to handle this.

And while the Disaster Recovery is proceeding, one can develop alternate venues for the project to continue its operations for various projects under your portfolio. The continuity of operations may be at a lower scale of efficiency, but at least your project will continue to be productive.

This is not a grandiose, or a pretentious, scheme. Consider a single developer - often developers will back-up their work, on an individual basis, so as to have a copy in case a disaster strikes, a networked drive, or their computer's drive gets corrupted. So, by that extension the project should also plan for and develop such capabilities.

The Disaster Recovery plan and the Continuity of Operations plan should become part of the project artifacts, which are exercised regularly and updated as needed.

# Train and Practice for Remote Operations and Teleworking

**TIME IS VALUABLE, AND TELEWORK IS A VIABLE COMPONENT TO HELP IMPROVE QUALITY OF LIFE IN MANY WAYS.**
~ *Rob Wittman*

Prepare and train your team to do telework and be able to perform remote operations, when and if necessary. This training and preparedness is essential in current day and times. Let us learn from the recent past when all over the world, people had to maintain a social distance and resort to working remotely, or teaching and learning remotely, where they could.

This requires your corporate culture to allow for it. Not just your project, but the company's infrastructure and security stance has to allow for this and support it. From the IT side the firewall and user authentication has to be robust enough to permit secure user access to the pertinent systems for users to be effective.

All the stakeholders should support it, if they do not, then you have to work on getting their concurrence and support.

These days, during and following the Pandemic, companies have had to learn to have their employees work remotely. Many companies have changed their Business Models to adapt to the personal space restrictions and social distancing. This has also opened the door to people living in one part of the country and working (remotely) in other parts of the country.

# Dealing with Overseas Clients or Corporate Partners

**COMMUNICATION IS THE KEY FOR ANY GLOBAL BUSINESS**
*~ Anita Roddick*

**ETIQUETTE**

Our contract at IBM was with the Civil Aviation Authority (CAA) of Britain. We had multiple sub-contractors on the project. These sub-contractors/partners were from various European countries.

We were cognizant of the time-differences between them and us and also between our clients in Britain and us (in USA). So, whenever we had conference call meetings with them and us, whether individually or in a group, we had to account for the differences. Usually the time difference between European countries and us was about 5-7 hours and while that did require making adjustments, it was not too much of a demand.

Besides the time difference, we also had to be sensitive to some cultural differences, country preferences and habits, terminology, idioms and language terms. After you learnt them, it was not very difficult. We still had to sensitive to these differences. Appreciating these differences and espousing them while dealing with people from those countries, it was always a pleasant surprise to them when we tried to adapt to these and made an effort to accommodate them.

All sub-contractors/partners particularly liked the fact that the CAA, when they hosted the in-person meetings, would offer the meeting attendees 'biscuits and tea' around 4:00 PM. This would boost our flagging attention after long and arduous meetings. We, at IBM, would reciprocate in a similar fashion when the CAA staff visited IBM in the US.

In the professional environment, the cultural differences are not that steep between the US and the European countries. So it is not very hard to adapt. However, when dealing with the far eastern countries, it is like one has entered a different world. Though the difference are becoming less pronounced as time passes and as the internet opens up communications and the borders. It also helps that the various countries are adapting cross-cultural ideas, habits, and languages. This blending is more evident in the younger generation – they being early adopters and early adapters.

For example, in the Japanese culture they are known to be very polite and famous for bowing as a greeting or farewell. Other far-eastern culture are known to treat their guests with great honor and respect.

I had also read an interesting incident in the Reader's Digest a long time back.  A Japanese company had won a contract from an American Company, to manufacture all-bearings for them.  Shortly after giving the contract to the Japanese company, a senior manager at the American company decided to visit the Japanese company for about a week.

When the Japanese corporate officers learnt that they forwarded a welcome and also sent this manager a package.  When the manager opened the package, he found a few ball bearings inside along with a pair of Chop-Sticks, made of metal handles with wooden stems.  The Metal handles had an intricate carved design, of the logo of the company.

There was also an accompanying note from the owner of the company telling this manager something along these lines 'Sir, we are overjoyed with your intention of visiting our county and the company.  We have included a set of ball bearings and a pair of chop-sticks.  Please find time to practice picking up the ball bearings with the chop-sticks.  Once you are able to do so comfortably and also put the ball bearings back in their box, without dropping them, you will know you are ready to enjoy a night out, dining on the exquisite Japanese cuisine, the same way as we Japanese do.  Thank you and we look forward to seeing you.'

**ONLY THOSE WHO WILL RISK GOING TOO FAR CAN POSSIBLY FIND OUT HOW FAR ONE CAN GO.**
*~ T.S. Eliot*

When dealing with overseas clients or contractors, one thing to be very cognizant about are the laws and regulations of that country.  The acceptable practices of other countries may be different.

When one is working for a large company, particularly a company with existing present, or past, contracts or dealings with that country, one can usually turn to the corporation for guidance. However it behooves one to understand the laws and regulations of the foreign country so one does not run afoul of them.

Dealing with and doing business with overseas clients has become easier these days due to most people being open to doing work online and the extensive use of the Internet for work and leisure. The pandemic has conditioned people to working remotely and online. We just have to make sure that we do not let our services deteriorate, like a lot of business are doing. People seem to find it convenient to claim that the pandemic is causing the decline in the quality of services they provide their clients.

Let us not forget that our clients are ones who help us put bread and butter on our plates and they are an important resource.

# Remember 'It is only a Job', but don't forget, 'It is the only Job you have'

### MY LIFE IS MY MESSAGE
### ~ *Mahatma Gandhi*

**Work Life Balance**

There has to be a balance between your professional life and your personal life. So, do not immerse yourself in your job to the extent that you neglect life, family, friends, hobbies, etc. Everything in our lives has a place and its own importance. Neglecting something, for extended periods of time, has dire consequences.

At the same time do not let your job affect your health or wellbeing by being too engrossed in its execution. Treat your job as just a job, but remember it pays your bills, and your client deserves what she/he paid for, and where possible give greater value to your client. Your client will be compelled to consider giving you additional business in the future.

**BALANCE YOUR LIFE WITH YOUR WORK**

So, your job has its proper place and it is very important to keep it in perspective, and your 'Life Balance' mindset ought to balance personal life with your professional life. Help your staff also cultivate such values.

As time passes, project deadlines approach, your job duties take on more importance. Once you have contributed to the meeting of your project commitments, the importance of other things in your life rises over the job. Never lose focus of your life and work, they have to be balanced for a fuller life.

Do not let job priorities always dictate how you spend your time in life and in performing day-to-day activities. There needs to be a balance.

It is said that 'Do what you love in life, then you will never have to work another day'. Are you happy in your job? Do you feel like going to work every morning? I had a consulting assignment once which I used to enjoy. The client was very good and understanding. The people around whom I worked very pleasant. Then the assignment finished.

The consulting job with the company, however did not come to an end. The company was happy with me, so they offered me another assignment, with a different department. I accepted the assignment. The new manager was terrible. He made life for the entire department terrible. Everyone, employees, other consultants and myself very unhappy working in that environment.

I had a choice to make, either quit, or continue. If I ended up quitting, that would be the end of my consulting assignments with that company. A consultant is loath to lose a client. So I stuck on for a while.

Every day it was becoming harder to be enthusiastic about going to work. I was on the edge all the time, like others in the department. I thought I had to change my environment. Change the job or change your attitude. I decided to tolerate for another few days, at least till the end of the pay period.

Luckily for me, things changed for the better, very quickly. Some employees had gone and complained to higher management a few days earlier. The company decided to remove this person from the management position of the department. And things rapidly improved for everyone.

So, if you do not enjoy your job – either change your job, or work on your attitude, till things improve. This is all part of 'Work Life Balance' as well.

# For every action – give it your 110 percent

**EXECUTE EVERY ACT OF THY LIFE AS THOUGH IT WERE THY LAST**
~ Marcus Aurelius

**THE KEY IS TO SET REALISTIC CUSTOMER EXPECTATIONS AND THEN TO EXCEED THEM, PREFERABLY IN UNEXPECTED AND HELPFUL WAYS.**
*~ Sir Richard Branson*

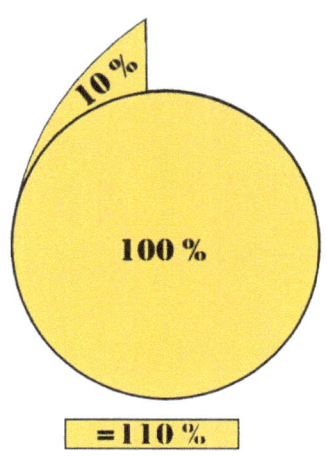

The master said – There are three categories of doctors. The Third category (lowest category) of doctor, examines the patient, diagnoses the condition and prescribes a course of action and a medicine – The doctor feels his/her job is done.

The Second category of doctor, examines the patient, diagnoses the condition and prescribes a medicine AND later checks on the patient whether the patient is taking the prescribed course of action and medicine. The First category (the best category) of doctor not only examines the patient, diagnoses the condition and prescribes a course of action and a medicine, but later *makes sure* that the patient is following the prescribed course of action and is indeed taking the medicine.

This example teaches me a lot. How can one give more that 100%? Completing a project delivery with agreed to functionality, without defects, on time, within budget, without exceeding allocated resources and agreed to support is by Project Management standards meeting your project goals 100%.

Going over the top, beyond that 100% would be actions like:
- Following up with the customer on the customer's satisfaction
- Ensuring that the product delivered is open-ended and modular (where it can be helped) to support future expansion
- Being flexible and proactive during the project execution
- Working collaboratively and pleasantly with all stakeholders
- Providing for training (where the project permits) to help the customer.

Going beyond 100% also includes:
- Taking care of your team
- Taking care of your corporate management to ensure all round satisfaction

All this is part of your 110% - going beyond and above the call-of-duty (so to say).

This is an attitude, a work ethic, and a welcome part of one's psyche. One should strive to cultivate such an attitude, so that all the stakeholders (customer, corporate management, staff, team, vendors, and end users) want to work with you now, and in the future (if they can help it).

We had a new Client Manager. He was the Project Director and he recognized our team's capabilities early on. We worked on a project to provide a green foot-print to the Client. Their nationwide, and overseas, hardware was due for replacement. We replaced their hardware and also virtualized their environment.

During the execution of the project we were able to utilize some efficiencies which were cost and time saving. This resulted in our completing the project ahead of scheduled time as well. To the client's credit, their end-users were also helpful due to our collaborative approach.

We did something unusual for the client.

As mentioned before, we returned the savings to the client on a fixed-price, pre-approved Statement of Work (SOW) back to the client, to be used at their discretion on other needed things. This was the extra 10% in the 110%.

The client appreciated it, so-much-so that they would find every opportunity to have my team handle (work on) new projects, or even tackle sticky problems. The client would subtly ask the upper management of my company to allow my team to tackle, or work, on the project. The upper management of our company would do their best to accommodate the client's wishes. And our team was always gainfully employed despite cuts and end-of-project cost saving measures.

# Become the 'Go-To' person

**IT'S GOING TO BE HARD, BUT HARD DOES NOT MEAN IMPOSSIBLE.**
*~ Success.com*

Try to be the person one would 'Go-To' if one needed answers to professional, or even personal, questions (remember personal issues do impact professional performance, and ultimately affect the project). Or if one needs help on project matters.

It takes time to become such a person.  One has to cultivate sincerity in one's work and dedication to corporate wellbeing and empathy for humanity.  Everyone is struggling to become successful, but it can never be at the cost of others.

From a project perspective, and as a manager, or an aspiring manager, work on knowing, not just your personal deadlines, but those of your team and your project, or program.  Become aware of project/program scope and potential issues so that you can recommend or take corrective action ahead of time.  Or even recommend it even if you are not a responsible actor for the task/project/program.

On my projects, I always had a specific 'go-to' person in mind for various, and specific, tasks.  Amongst various engineers there was one engineer who was the fixer for various engineering problems.  I promoted that person as a chief engineer.

I also had a person in mind for resolving Configuration Management issues. That person only wanted a higher salary – she got it. There was a person who could do any professional task he was asked to do. He was thorough and methodical, documented all steps, got everyone involved and on board – his past managers failed to recognize his talent and he was not appreciated or compensated. On my project, he was given appreciation and compensation since he well deserved it. And he appreciated that recognition and due to that he tried even harder.

Over time these people shone in their respective areas and were given greater responsibilities and recognition.

There is always the other side of the coin in every case and so there is one here too. Once people recognize this trait in you, they will try to load you with more work. Extra work should not worry you, unless it is affecting your work-life balance. Extra work means more opportunities to learn and a chance to expand your horizons.

When I started working on my first job, I was still learning the ins-and-outs of my job. I was very enthusiastic to learn and become proficient. I would jump in to start work on any task I was responsible for. Seeing this enthusiasm, the other engineers would kind of say 'Whoa, let us step back a little and let him tackle it'. I knew that they were shirking some of their responsibilities, but I did not mind. I was determined to excel in my work and understand the intricacies of my task, so that I could do them well. I also wanted to get over 'the rookie' adjective used behind my back.

This was the flip-side of the coin as I was on the fast track to becoming the Go-To-Guy. This has its own rewards as my senior engineers started relying more and more on me and would go out of the way to accommodate my requests, however trivial they may have been.

I have always maintained the attitude to learn what I need to and also go beyond my needed knowledge and skill. This I feel is the only way to excel in one's life.

# Some useful Project Management Formulae

**THE FORMULA FOR SUCCESS IS SIMPLE: PRACTICE AND CONCENTRATION THEN MORE PRACTICE AND MORE CONCENTRATION.**
*~ Babe Didrikson Zaharias*

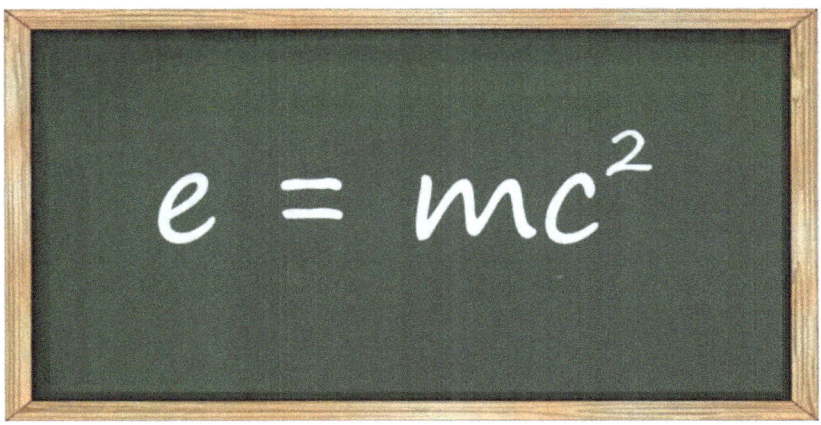

Here are some formulas for Project Management.  They are practical and useful in the Management Profession.  They are also useful if one desires to get credentialed.

| Actual Cost of Work Performed (ACWP) | Actual Cost (AC) |
|---|---|
| Budget at Completion (BAC) | Represents the original project budge |

| | |
|---|---|
| Budgeted Cost for Work Performed (BCWP) | Earned Value (EV) |
| Budgeted Cost for Work Scheduled (BCWS) | Present Value (PV) |
| Benefit Cost Ratio (BCR) | Bigger is better ((BCR or Benefit / Cost) revenue or Payback VS. Cost) Or PV or Revenue / PV of Cost |
| Range of Variance on Budget Estimate | -10% to +25% of Funds |
| Burn Rate (Is the rate at which the project is spending its original budget) | 1/CPI Where CPI = Cost performance Index |
| Communication Channels | N(N -1)/2 Where N = Number of Persons (team members/stakeholders) |
| Contract related formulas | Savings = Target Cost – Actual Cost<br><br>Bonus = Savings x Percentage<br><br>Contract Cost = Bonus + Fees<br><br>Total Cost = Actual Cost + Contract Cost |
| Cost Performance Index (CPI) | EV / AC |
| Cost Variance (CV) | EV - AC |
| Definitive Estimate | -5% to +10% |

| | |
|---|---|
| | Definitive Estimates are based on detailed information from each work package within the Work Breakdown Structure (WBS) or estimates completed at the activity level and are usually -5% to +10% accurate |
| Discounted Cash Flow | Cash Flow x Discount Factor |
| Earned Value (EV)<br><br>The measure of work completed expressed in  terms of the budget authorized for that work. | %Complete * BAC |
| Estimate At Completion (EAC) | BAC / CPI,<br>AC + ETC<br>(Initial Estimates are flawed)<br>AC + BAC – EV<br>(Future variances are not typical)<br>AC + (BAC - EV) / CPI<br>(Future Variance would be typical) |
| Estimate To Complete (ETC) | EAC - AC |
| Expected Monetary Value (EMV) | Probability * Impact |
| Float or Slack | LS-ES and LF-EF |
| Internal Rate of Return (IRR) | Bigger is better |
| Net Present Value (NPV) | Bigger is better |
| Order of Magnitude Estimate (ROM) | -25% to +75%<br>(-50 to +100% as per the PMBOK) |

| Payback Period | Less is better Net Investment / Avg. Annual cash flow. |
|---|---|
| Percentage complete | EV / BAC |
| PERT | (Pessimistic Estimate + (4 x Most Likely Estimate) + Optimistic Estimate) / 6 |
| Point of Total Assumption (PTA) | ((Ceiling Price - Target Price)/buyer's Share Ratio) + Target Cost |
| Present Value PV | FV / ((1 + r)^term) |
| Return on Assets ( ROA ) | NEBT / Total Assets OR NEAT / Total Assets |
| Return on Investment ( ROI ) | NEBT / Total Investment OR NEAT / Total Investment |
| Return on Sales ( ROS ) | Net Income Before Taxes (NEBT) / Total Sales OR Net Income After Taxes ( NEAT ) / Total Sales |
| Schedule Performance Index (SPI) | EV / PV In other words it is the Earned Schedule (ES) Divided by the Actual Time (AT) |
| Schedule Variance (SV) | EV - PV |
| Sigma σ | 1σ = 68.27% 2σ = 95.45% 3σ = 99.73% 6σ = 99.99985% |
| Standard Deviation (SD) (σ) | (P - O) / 6 |

| | |
|---|---|
| To Complete Performance Index TCPI | ( BAC - EV ) / ( BAC - AC ) Values for the TCPI index of less than 1.0 is good because it indicates the efficiency to complete is less than planned. How efficient must the project team be to complete the remaining work with the remaining money? |
| Variance | [(P - O)/6 ] squared |
| Variation At Completion (VAC) | BAC - EAC |
| Working Capital | Current Assets - Current Liabilities

It is a measure of short-term liquidity of the project |

# Some Book Titles worth consideration

**READING IS ESSENTIAL FOR THOSE WHO SEEK TO RISE ABOVE THE ORDINARY.**
*~ Jim Rohn*

Here are some books which opened up my thinking. I do not necessarily agree with each author 100% in everything they have written, but I have found nuggets in each one of these books:

- How to win Friends & Influence People Paperback – January 1, 2011
    By Dale Carnegie (Author)

- Looking Out for #1: How to Get from Where You Are Now to Where You Want to Be in Life Paperback – November 6, 2013
    By Robert Ringer (Author)

- The Wisdom of Baltasar Gracian: A Practical Manual for
Good and Perilous Times Paperback – December 1, 1992
  By Baltasar Gracian Y Morales (Author), Adapted
and Edited by J. Leonard Kaye (Editor)

- Be an Extraordinary Person in an Ordinary World
Orient Paperbacks, 2008
  By Dr. Robert H. Schuller

- A Guide to the Project Management Body of Knowledge
(PMBOK® Guide) Get the latest Edition
  By Project Management Institute

- Think and Grow Rich: The Landmark Bestseller Now
Revised and Updated for the 21st Century (Think and
Grow Rich Series) Paperback – August 18, 2005
  By Napoleon Hill (Author)

# I have learned….

**EVERYONE YOU WILL EVER MEET KNOWS SOMETHING YOU DON'T**
*~ Bill Nye*

I have learned a lot from people around me.  Some have been elders, others more experienced, some have been peers, and many have been younger to me.  I want to acknowledge those people by first name and the quality I have tried to inculcate from them.  When those people read their names and the quality/qualities I have observed in them, they will (hopefully) recognize themselves mentioned here and be encouraged to impart those qualities to others.

I am using only first names and request my elders to overlook this form of address.

| Name of Person | Quality(s) |
| --- | --- |
| Abhijeet | People Skills |
| Arun | Practical Wisdom |
| Ash | Natural artistic talent, acquired business sense |
| Bhagwanti | Love and care for people |
| Dipesh | Helpful Nature |
| Eric | Engineering Knowhow and enjoying it |
| Gunjan | Dedication |
| Ishwari | Worldly Wisdom |
| Jitender | Business acumen and photography art |
| Kanchan | Job dedication |
| Kiran | Sweet Nature |
| Krishna | Simplicity |
| Manju | Persistence |
| Manohar | All Rounder |
| Marv | Ability to make a person feel important |
| Mohini | Persistence |
| My Father | Wisdom, Absolute Truthfulness, Hard Work |
| My Mother | Love for All living beings, very big heart |
| Neeraj | Humanity |
| Nikhil | Entrepreneur |
| Pratap | Following his inner rhythm |
| Rajeev | Hard work |
| Ravi | Compassion and Hard work |
| Ray | Integrity and Loyalty |
| Rohit | Pattern Recognition |
| Ruchika | Pleasant Nature |
| Shivani | Boldness |
| Shyam | Spirituality |
| Sonia | Determination |
| Sujata | Caring for others |
| Usha | Always Cheerful and positive thinking |
| Veena | Dedication to job |
| Yogindra | Belief in Self |

# Parting Words

Let me share some words my father often recited to inspire me (from the poem 'The Psalm of Life' by Henry Wadsworth Longfellow):

**LIVES OF GREAT MEN ALL REMIND US**
**WE CAN MAKE OUR LIVES SUBLIME,**
**AND, DEPARTING, LEAVE BEHIND US**
**FOOTPRINTS ON THE SANDS OF TIME;**

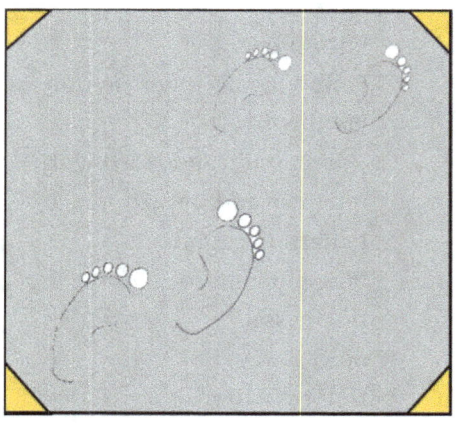

# Index

www.ingramcontent.com/pod-product-compliance
Lightning Source LLC
Chambersburg PA
CBHW060913120626
46553CB00001B/305